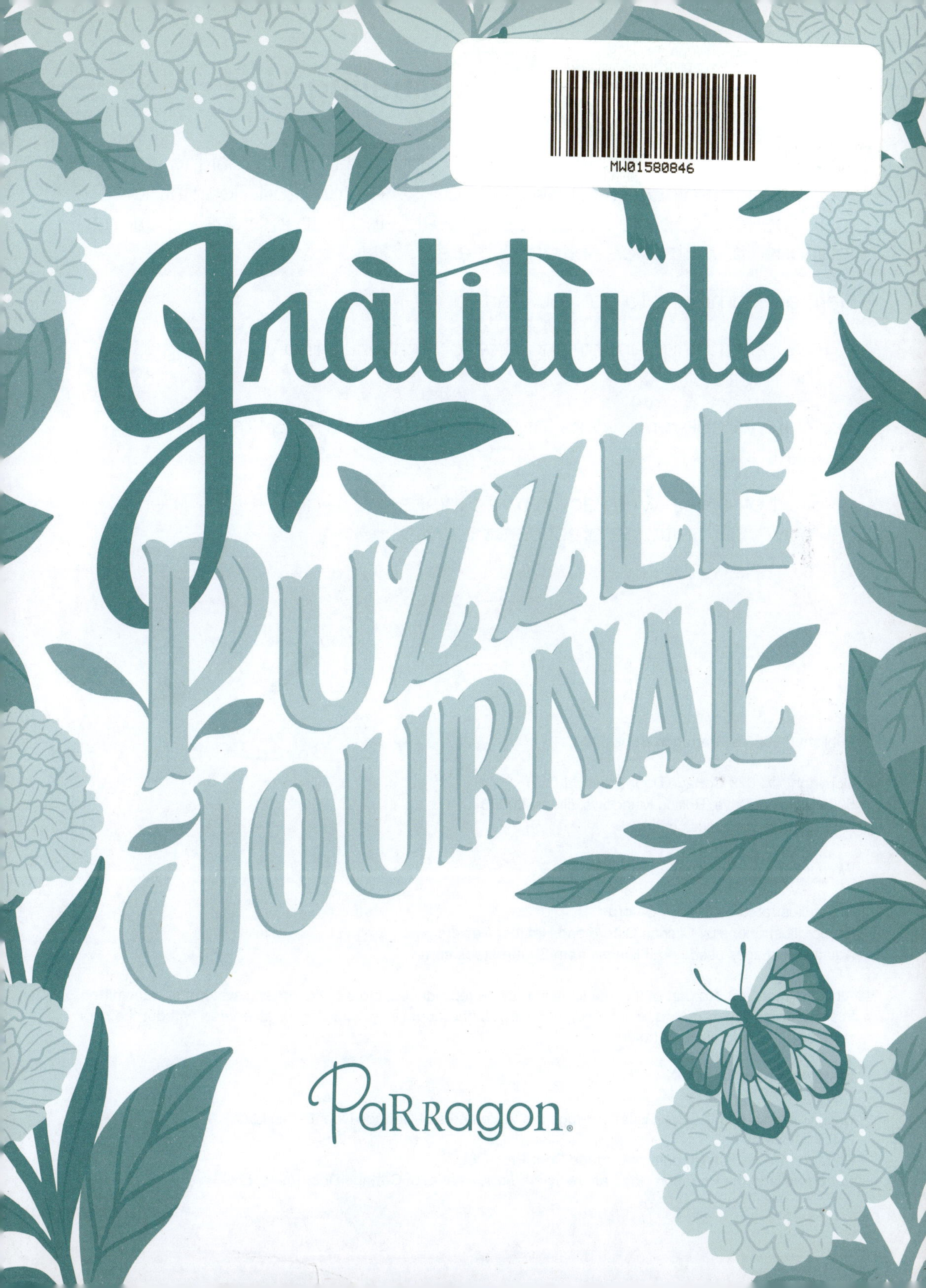

Gratitude
PUZZLE
JOURNAL
PaRragon

Gratitude Journaling Tips

There are many benefits to gratitude journaling beyond making you feel better! Studies have shown that consistent gratitude journaling can foster better sleep, decrease stress levels, and help improve emotional relationships with one's self and others.

Here are some tips to get you started:

- Choose the right journaling method that will keep you engaged in the habit.

- Write whenever it works for you! There is no wrong time to find gratitude.

- Start off small. Write down three things you're grateful for. Then grow your gratitude practice as you can.

Published 2023 by Parragon Books, Ltd.

Copyright © 2023 Cottage Door Press, LLC
5005 Newport Drive, Rolling Meadows, Illinois 60008
www.cottagedoorpress.com

Word search puzzles created by diacriTech

Cover illustrated by Clairice Gifford
Interior illustrations by Clairice Gifford and Heather Powers
Additional images used under license from Shutterstock.com

ISBN: 978-1-64638-911-7

Brain Busters™ and the Brain Busters™ logo are trademarks of Cottage Door Press, LLC.

Parragon Books is an imprint of Cottage Door Press, LLC.
Parragon® and the Parragon® logo are registered trademarks of Cottage Door Press, LLC.

Using this Book

This book includes journaling prompts and several kinds of puzzles. The prompts will guide your gratitude practice month-by-month. Solving the gratitude-themed puzzles will inspire mindfulness and help you set aside time to be present and reflect on for whom and what you are thankful.

How to solve the puzzles:

Cryptogram

Use the clue letters to solve the encrypted gratitude-themed message. Hint: look for one-letter words and repeated letter patterns.

Letter Circle

How many words can you find in the letter circle? Every word must use the center letter plus two or more of the other letters. No letter can be used more than once in a single word. There is at least one word that uses all of the letters in the circle.

Maze

Start at one arrow and draw a line to the second arrow without crossing through any of the maze walls.

Word Scramble

Rearrange the letters to find the original words, using the title above as a clue for the theme of the scrambled words.

Word Search

Find and circle the search terms in the puzzle. Words can be found forward, backward, vertically, and diagonally. Sometimes the words overlap.

List one big goal you'd like to accomplish this month:

____

____

____

____

What are some emotions you'd like to let go of this month?	What are some emotions you'd like to carry into this month?
•	•
•	•
•	•
•	•
•	•

Write some positive affirmations you can use throughout the month:

1. ____

2. ____

3. ____

Show Gratitude

ACKNOWLEDGE	KINDNESS	SERVICE
COMPLIMENT	LETTER	SMILE
GIFT	LISTEN	TEXT
HUG	PHONE CALL	VISIT
JOURNAL	PRAY	WORDS

Cryptogram Quote

A	B	C	D	E	F	G	H	I	J	K	L	M
				A								

N	O	P	Q	R	S	T	U	V	W	X	Y	Z
				N								

```
_ _ _ _E_   _ _ _ _ _ _E_ _E_S_ _S_   _ _S_
M J I A     P T J Q Y F A S A N N     Y N

  _ _E_    _ _ _   _ _ _   _S_ _,_
  H B A S  V T I   G D S   N D V

"_ _ _ _ _   _ _ _   _ _ _E_
 M B D S C   V T I   P T J   M B A

 _E_ _ _E_ _ _E_ _ _E_."
 A Z X A J Y A S G A
```

—Oprah

Calming Instruments

CIMHE ⬚⬚⬚⬚⬚

UTFEL ⬚⬚⬚⬚⬚

RGUTAI ⬚⬚⬚⬚⬚⬚

APHR ⬚⬚⬚⬚

PAOIN ⬚⬚⬚⬚⬚

IINGSNG OBLW ⬚⬚⬚⬚⬚⬚ ⬚⬚⬚⬚

EGRLNITA ⬚⬚⬚⬚⬚⬚⬚⬚

EULKELU ⬚⬚⬚⬚⬚⬚⬚

Letter Circle

Monthly Vision Board

A vision board is a visual reminder of your goals and intentions. Inspire yourself and create a monthly vision board using this page to collage, doodle, sketch...or all of the above!

I Am Grateful for...

ANIMALS	FOOD	MOVEMENT
EDUCATION	FRIENDS	PARTNER
FAITH	HEALTH	SCHOOL
FAMILY	HOME	SHELTER

Cryptogram Quote

A	B	C	D	E	F	G	H	I	J	K	L	M
				X								

N	O	P	Q	R	S	T	U	V	W	X	Y	Z
							G					

```
_ E _   _ _ _ U _ _ _       _ E _ _ _ _ _ _ _ _ _ _
P X     K A B G L M         R X I J H Q V L Y

_ _ U _ _ _   _ _ U _   _ _ _ E _ _ _ _ _ _ _ _ ,
R B G V J     B G I     O L X K K Q V W K

_ U _ _   _ E _   _ _ _ U _ _ _       _ _ _ _ _
O G J     P X     K A B G L M         H L K B

_ _ E _ _   _ _ U _   _ _ _ E _ _ _ _ _ _ _ _
C H E X     B G I     O L X K K Q V W K

_ _ U _ _ _ .
R B G V J
```

—Neal A. Maxwell

A Good Night's Sleep

DNWO MRERTOOCF

JAPAAMS

MNONEAILT

NEAERLVD

DMESRA

LKIS EHETSS

TUNROEI

TWIHE OEISN

Letter Circle

Positive Intentions

FLOW	INTENT	READ
FORGIVE	LET GO	SAFE
GRACE	LOVE	SLEEP
GRATITUDE	MINDSET	WELL-BEING
HEALTH	PRACTICE	WHISPER
	PRIORITIZE	

Write about a significant event in your life. What did you learn from it?
Are you grateful for having experienced it?

Nature Walk

TCCOELL

KECER

RSASG

NIEYFTID

IHKE

ALSEEV

EMWODA

SDBRI

Letter Circle

Comforts of Home

RNUGNNI ARETW ⬜⬜⬜⬜⬜⬜⬜ ⬜⬜⬜⬜⬜

ARI TNGODICIOINN ⬜⬜⬜ ⬜⬜⬜⬜⬜⬜⬜⬜⬜⬜

LSINEAPPCA ⬜⬜⬜⬜⬜⬜⬜⬜⬜

ORHTMOAB ⬜⬜⬜⬜⬜⬜⬜⬜

YFLAIM ⬜⬜⬜⬜⬜⬜

EATH ⬜⬜⬜⬜

RTCLYIIECTE ⬜⬜⬜⬜⬜⬜⬜⬜⬜⬜⬜

OSHERW ⬜⬜⬜⬜⬜⬜

Letter Circle

____

____

____

______________________   ______________________

______________________   ______________________

______________________   ______________________

Grateful in Other Languages

AGRADECIDA	GRATA	RECONNAISSANTE
ARIGATAI	GRATUS	SHAKIR
BERSYUKUR	KIITOLLINEN	TACKSAM
BUÍOCH	MAHALO	TAINGEIL
DANKBAAR	MINNETTAR	

Cryptogram Quote

A	B	C	D	E	F	G	H	I	J	K	L	M

N	O	P	Q	R	S	T	U	V	W	X	Y	Z
				V	U							

```
  R                    S
_ _ _ _ _ _ _ _ _   _ _   _ _ _
C V G A B A M O Z   B U   W H A

                      R           S
_ _ _ _   _ _ _   _ _ _ _ _ _ _ _
H W P F   A I Z   C V Z G A Z U A

          R             S,
_ _   _ _ _ _ _ _ _   _ _ _   _ _ _
H R   T B V A M Z U   L M A   A I Z

        R
_ _ _ _ _ _   _ _   _ _ _
J G V Z W A   H R   G P P

          R S.
_ _ _ _ _ _ _ _ .
H A I Z V U
```

—Marcus Tullius Cicero

Memory Lane

RDEANMGI

ASGTLIOAN

RMEBEMER

NPREDO

ARCELL

IEMCERSIN

IEITSVR

CBSHKALAF

Letter Circle

Journal Here

MAEPTANTR

AARYCKBD

BERDOOM

OCHCU

BEATL

CTKHEIN

YIBARLR

LNOEIN

Letter Circle

N
S O
I E A
G Y G

Rhymes with Gratitude

ALLUDE

ATTITUDE

BARBECUED

BROOD

DELUDE

EXUDE

FEUD

FOOD

INCLUDE

INTRUDE

LONGITUDE

MOOD

PLATITUDE

SCREWED

VIEWED

Cryptogram Quote

A	B	C	D	E	F	G	H	I	J	K	L	M
				G							S	

N	O	P	Q	R	S	T	U	V	W	X	Y	Z

```
_ E _ _      _ _ _ _ _ _ _ _ _ E    _ L _ E
C G A T      H T A E M E Q J G      S M P G

_    _ L _ _ _ ,  _ _ _    _ _    _ _ L _ L
A    I S V A P    A X J    M E    C M S S

_ E _ E _    _ E _ E _    _ _ _ _ _ E _    _ _
O G G J      G Y G T D    I V T X G T      V O

_ _ _ _    _ L _ _ E .
D V Q T    S M O G
```

—Rumi

 # Monthly Gratitude Reflections 

List five things you're grateful for this month:

1. ____

2. ____

3. ____

4. ____

5. ____

<table>
<tr>
<td>

Write about one experience you had this month that you're especially grateful for:

</td>
<td>

List some people in your life that made you feel loved this month:

</td>
</tr>
</table>

 # Monthly Plans and Goals 

List one big goal you'd like to accomplish this month:

____

____

____

____

What are some emotions you'd like to let go of this month?

-
-
-
-
-

What are some emotions you'd like to carry into this month?

-
-
-
-
-

Write some positive affirmations you can use throughout the month:

1. ____

2. ____

3. ____

THINK
POSITIVE

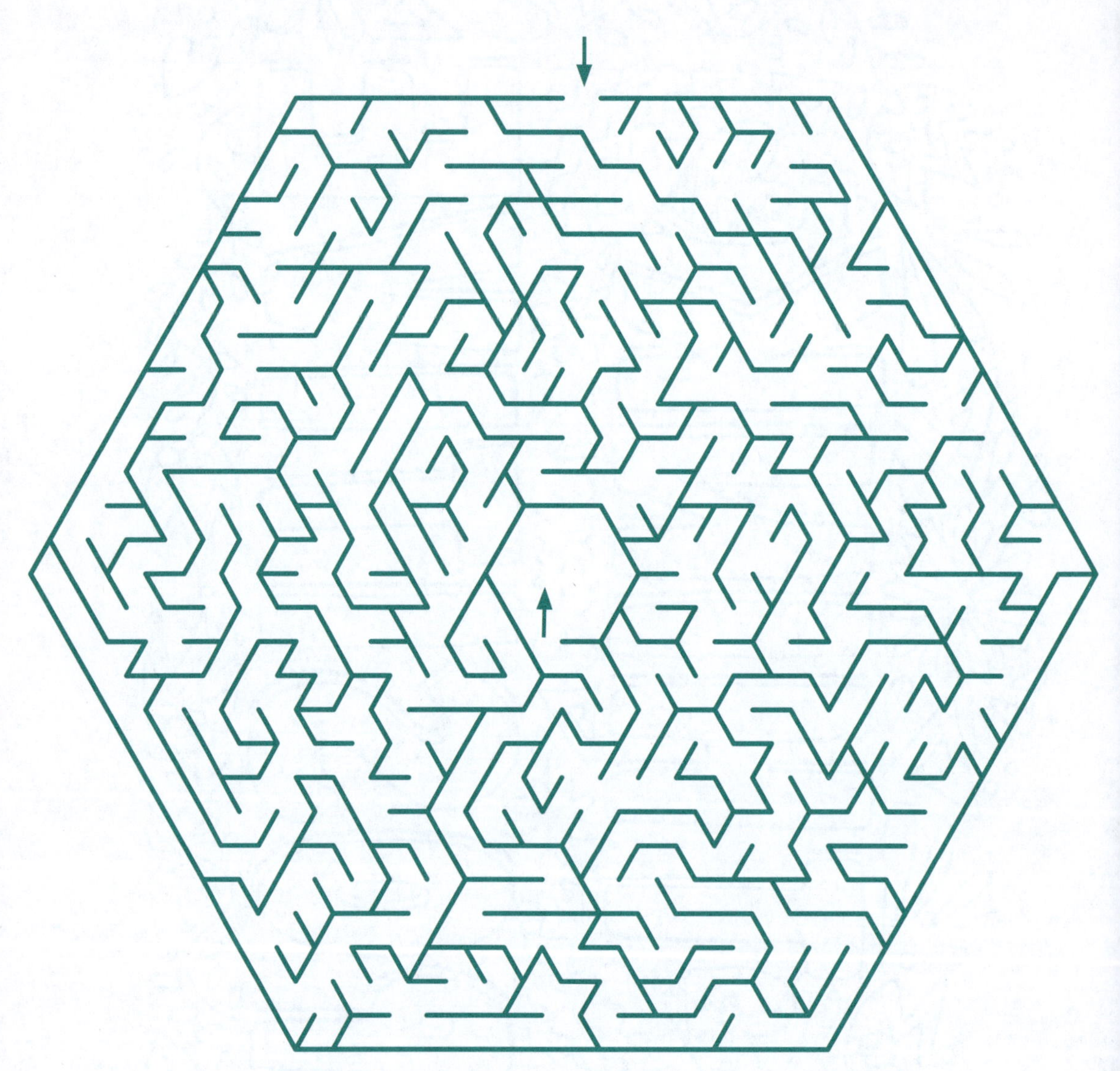

Opposite of Stress

CEACTP

CTRFOOM

AOOSNIOLNTC

RDRISEGAD

NEREUD

NIMANITMZIIO

AXLRE

TNSUEDAERT

Letter Circle

Self-actualization

CSCAOMLHPI

DERIV

LLLFFUI

THGWOR

MWAOSL

OLETPAITN

RAEHC

RALIATIOZNE

Letter Circle

Monthly Vision Board

A vision board is a visual reminder of your goals and intentions. Inspire yourself and create a monthly vision board using this page to collage, doodle, sketch...or all of the above!

Thankful for Nature

BLOOMS

BREEZE

CLEAN AIR

CREATURES

FOREST

FRESH SNOW

GREEN TREES

LEAVES

OCEAN

PARK

PLANTS

RAINBOW

STARS

SUN-SHOWER

SUNSHINE

Cryptogram Quote

A	B	C	D	E	F	G	H	I	J	K	L	M
W												

N	O	P	Q	R	S	T	U	V	W	X	Y	Z
					U							

"T A _ _ _ _ _ _ _" _ _ _ T
 U Y W Z P   N L E   I X   U Y K

_ _ _ T _ _ _ A _ _ _ T _ A T
H K X U   B G W N K G   U Y W U

A _ _ _ _ _ _ _ _ _ _ _ A _ .
W Z N L Z K   R L E S M   X W N

—Alice Walker

Types of Dreams

EADRMYDA

GLLIFNA

LNGIYF

EBNIG ETAL

KEADN

AMIHRGNTE

IMPOEIONNTR

ITGKNA SETT

Letter Circle

Positive Affirmations

BE KIND	FREE OF WORRY	PROUD
BEAUTIFUL	GREAT DAY	SMART
BELIEVE	I SEE	STRONG
BOLD	JOURNEY	TRUST
BRAVE	LOVED	WORTHY
	MY BEST	

Cryptogram Quote

A	B	C	D	E	F	G	H	I	J	K	L	M

N	O	P	Q	R	S	T	U	V	W	X	Y	Z
E						B						

<pre>
 T   T   T
 B M L   K F R N   B M Q B   Z H A L K

     T   N   N   N
     B M Q E X K   C Q E   S H E D

                 T   N   T   N
 C F T S F G B   H E   L A L G W B M H E Z ;

     T   T   T
     B M L   K F R N   B M Q B

                     N   N   N
 C F T O N Q H E K   C Q E   S H E D

                 T   N   N   T   N
 C F T S F G B   H E   E F B M H E Z .
</pre>

—Hannah Whitall Smith

In Good Health

BREATHE	GOOD BREATH	SIGHT
DEWY SKIN	HAPPY	STRONG NAILS
ENERGY	HEALTHY HAIR	TASTE
FEELING	HEARING	TOUCH
	RESTED	

Have a Grateful Day

EDPE HREBTA

KAEM EDB

TEIRUGDAT ILTS

ROESBEV

IRUNHOS

WORSHE

EOIFGRV

OG LKAW

Letter Circle

D
T   N
M
S   E
I

Celebrations

CARNIVAL	HOLI	RAMADAN
CHRISTMAS	MARDI GRAS	ST. PATRICK'S
EASTER	OKTOBERFEST	THANKSGIVING
HALLOWEEN	PASSOVER	VALENTINES
HANUKKAH	PURIM	YEE PENG

Cryptogram Quote

A	B	C	D	E	F	G	H	I	J	K	L	M
	N			S								

N	O	P	Q	R	S	T	U	V	W	X	Y	Z

```
_ _ _ _ _ _ _ _ E _   _ _   _   B _ _
Y M A Q I Q F C S      I D   A   N I Y

_ _ _ _ _.   _ _   _ _ _ _   _ _ _   _ _
Q V I U Y    I Q   W F Q D   R K F   I U

_   _ _ _ _ E _   _ _ E _ E _   _ _ _ _'_ E
A   W T A B S     E V S M S     R K F M S

_ _ _ B _ E.
V F O N T S
```

— Andra Day

TEA TIME

Mindfulness

SINSUCOCO

NLTISE

EEIDMATT

EPATICNE

AUESP

PCEAE

ETPSERN

DERSAC

Letter Circle

Magnificent Sky

ECRNUEAL

LEYLOW

HEEBSRT

GERONA

IPKN

ROYS

TTCONO AYNDC

LLCIA

Letter Circle

Thankful for Furry and Feathered Friends

BIRD	GUINEA PIG	PARROT
CHICKEN	HAMSTER	PUPPY
FERRET	HORSE	RABBIT
GERBIL	KITTEN	RAT
GOAT	MOUSE	

Cryptogram Quote

A	B	C	D	E	F	G	H	I	J	K	L	M

N	O	P	Q	R	S	T	U	V	W	X	Y	Z
J							Z					

       '   N   N   N

P V N T N W   J X P V Q J M   J Q H N T

      N   U N

P V R J   Z J N K S N H P N L

R S S T N H Q R P Q X J   Q I

   U'   U

E X Z T N   M T R P N I Z C ,   M N P

      N

R   S N J .

—Helen Ellis

 # Monthly Gratitude Reflections 

List five things you're grateful for this month:

1. ____

2. ____

3. ____

4. ____

5. ____

Write about one experience you had this month that you're especially grateful for:

List some people in your life that made you feel loved this month:

 # Monthly Plans and Goals 

List one big goal you'd like to accomplish this month:

____

____

____

____

What are some emotions you'd like to let go of this month?

-
-
-
-
-

What are some emotions you'd like to carry into this month?

-
-
-
-
-

Write some positive affirmations you can use throughout the month:

1. ____

2. ____

3. ____

Positive Words

ACCEPTING	COMPLIMENTARY	SUPPORTIVE
ADMIRE	FAVORABLE	SURE
ADORE	FLATTER	SYMPATHETIC
CERTAIN	FRIENDLY	WARM
CLEAR	GOOD	WORSHIP
	PRAISE	

Self-care Kit

ZCYO SSKOC

READ-EER

FEAC KMSA

LAROUJN

TOFS CISMU

LTEAKNB

OGYA AMT

OKBO

Letter Circle

Cryptogram Quote

A	B	C	D	E	F	G	H	I	J	K	L	M
						E					K	

N	O	P	Q	R	S	T	U	V	W	X	Y	Z

G\
E Q D Z F Z S W L   G\
E Y L R

I L P Y U W   Z J L   " B F U L   D U W

" Z J F U L "   D U W   L\
N K D F B R   Z J L

Z Q S Z J   Z J D Z   L L\
D K K   Y G

L\
K F G L   F R   D   H S Q L   G\
E F G Z.

—Henri J. M. Nouwen

Monthly Vision Board

A vision board is a visual reminder of your goals and intentions. Inspire yourself and create a monthly vision board using this page to collage, doodle, sketch...or all of the above!

Stay in the Present

NEIGB

BANTHERIG

RTCURNE

XNTEIETS

ILDNFMU

OEBRSVE

DYOAT

VLGIIN

Letter Circle

Mindful of Others

ACKNOWLEDGE	GIVE	LOVE
ATTENTIVE	HELPFUL	RESPECT
BOUNDARY	IMPACT	THOUGHTFUL
CARE	INTENT	TRAVEL
CONSIDERATE	INVOLVEMENT	VOLUNTEER
	LISTEN	

Cryptogram Quote

A	B	C	D	E	F	G	H	I	J	K	L	M
E				S								

N	O	P	Q	R	S	T	U	V	W	X	Y	Z

```
_ _ E _      _ E A _ _ _ _      _ _ _ _ _ ,
K Q S C      S E O I C V        Y R J I O

_ E _ E _ _ E _      _ _ E      _ _ E      _ _ _
R S G S G N S R      O Q S      T C S      K Q T

_ A _ _ E _ _      _ _ E      _ _ E E .
D B E C O S H       O Q S      O R S S
```

—Vietnamese Proverb

Rhymes with Chill

ALFODDFI

LLIRD

IITLLNS

FLIUFLL

HLOMILEL

LUQARITN

LMIIDLWN

LREIFL

Letter Circle

Cryptogram Quote

A	B	C	D	E	F	G	H	I	J	K	L	M
				X								

N	O	P	Q	R	S	T	U	V	W	X	Y	Z
		M			W							

```
    _ _ _ T _ T _ _ E _    _ _    _ T _ E
    T Y A W F W H O X      F S    W D X

              _ T _ _ _ T
              A Z F P F W G   W N

 E _ P E _   _ E _ _   _ E _    _ _ _
 X L M X Y F X C V X   P F Q X  A S   A

    _ _ _ _ T.  _ _ T   _ _ _ _ E _   _ _ T E
    T F Q W     F W     P F Z X Y A W X S  H S

    _ _ _ _   _ T _ E _   _ P _   _ _
    Q Y N B   W D X       M Y F S N C  N Q

    _ _ E _ - _ P _ E _   _ _ _ _ P _ T _ _.
    S X P Q   M Y X N V V H M A W F N C
```

— John Ortberg

Types of Prayer

ADORATION	FAITH	PSALM
AGREEMENT	FORGIVENESS	REQUEST
CONFESSION	GUIDANCE	REVELATION
CONTRITION	LAMENT	THANKSGIVING
DELIVERANCE	PETITION	VOW
	PRAISE	

Self-care Day

ACTFR

SEAAMSG

OSERWH

EHATYRP

BEAK

EGGNDIRAN

ADSPTCO

ONCYISAATT

Letter Circle

T F D I G E A R I

Cryptogram Quote

A	B	C	D	E	F	G	H	I	J	K	L	M
								O				

N	O	P	Q	R	S	T	U	V	W	X	Y	Z
	L											

```
 I        O              I           O          I
___  _________  ________  _________  ________
 O   D I L N P  R E O Z   X L S F O F C

              I              O
         ________  ________
          I O R E   A P Q L W R

          I     I               O
________________  _______  _____
R E D F N Z C O Q O F C   H L S   X K

     I                O
__________,  ______  ______  ____
H S O P F A Z   R E P   L Y A   D F A

______  _____.
R E P   F P I
```

YOU
MATTER

Intuition

NITCOGONI

HGISTNI

INCTNIST

GEELOWKND

CREPETP

NTNORIIMEPO

ILNAAOTR

EESNS

Letter Circle

Cryptogram Quote

A	B	C	D	E	F	G	H	I	J	K	L	M
P						I						

N	O	P	Q	R	S	T	U	V	W	X	Y	Z
					Y							

_ _G_ _ _ _ _ _ _ _ _ _ _ _ _ _A_
A C I U J W   N M W C S J T   W R P W

_ _ _ _ _ _ _ _G_ _ _ _ _A_ _ _A_
J G J N   W R M Z I R   R J   R P T   P

_ _ _ _ _S_ _A_ _ _ _ _ _A_ _ _', _ _
G J X K   Y F P U U   R J P X W   C W

_ _ _ _ _ _ _ _ _A_ _A_ _ _ _ _
S M Z U T   R M U T   P   X P W R J X

_ _A_ _G_ _ _A_ _ _ _ _ _
U P X I J   P F M Z N W   M H

_G_ _A_ _ _ _ _ _ _ _ _.
I X P W C W Z T J

— A. A. Milne

Dream Journal

CAPTURE	MESSAGE	SYMBOL
ENTRY	MORNING	UNLOCK
FRAGMENT	NIGHTMARE	WAKE UP
MEANING	RECORD	WAKING LIFE
MEMORY	REMEMBER	WRITE
	SUBCONSCIOUS	

The Divine in Me...

EATASMN

UNHDI

NROOH

HLTGI

YGAO

UUOSNOCSISCB

APHERS

RASNKTIS

Letter Circle

 # Monthly Gratitude Reflections

List five things you're grateful for this month:

1. ____

2. ____

3. ____

4. ____

5. ____

Write about one experience you had this month that you're especially grateful for:

List some people in your life that made you feel loved this month:

Monthly Plans and Goals

List one big goal you'd like to accomplish this month:

____

____

____

____

What are some emotions you'd like to let go of this month?

-
-
-
-
-

What are some emotions you'd like to carry into this month?

-
-
-
-
-

Write some positive affirmations you can use throughout the month:

1. ____

2. ____

3. ____

Mindfulness Exercises

ACCEPTANCE	EAT	MEDITATION
AWARENESS	FIND JOY	MOVE
BE PRESENT	FOCUS	PAUSE
BODY SCAN	GRATITUDE	WALK
BREATHING	HYDRATE	WORKOUT
	LISTENING	

Spa Day

FCAILA

DYR SRBHU

EEMSSSUA

UMD HBTA

SNUAA

BUCRS

DEESWEA PARW

CYLA KMSA

Letter Circle

Cryptogram Quote

A	B	C	D	E	F	G	H	I	J	K	L	M
X												

N	O	P	Q	R	S	T	U	V	W	X	Y	Z
											W	

```
__ Y_ __   __ __ __      __ __ __    __ __    __ __ __ A_ __ __
L  G       W  P  U       M  H  H      J  P      N  H  X  M  P  J

__ __ __   __ __ __ __ __    __ __ A_ __ __ ,
G  P  N     R  L  K  L  J  R    C  B  X  J  D  M

__ __ __   A_ __ __ __    __ __ __ __    __ __ __ Y_
C  B  H     G  X  U  V  C    V  L  H  M     P  J  V  W

__ __ __   Y_ __ __ __ __ __ __ __ __ .
L  J       W  P  U  N  M  H  V  G
```

— Tecumseh

Monthly Vision Board

A vision board is a visual reminder of your goals and intentions. Inspire yourself and create a monthly vision board using this page to collage, doodle, sketch...or all of the above!

Enlighten Me

BAOSBR

ERSSNAWEA

TTILVCAEU

OREVIPM

TIIGNSH

IOPEPNTCER

IZALEER

OELKDENWG

Letter Circle

D I A
D T T E
E M

Mindful Movement

BELLY BREATHE	PILATES	SWAY
BEND	QIGONG	TAI CHI
DANCE	REACH	TWIST
EXTEND	SMILE	WALK
LIFT	STAND	YOGA
	STRETCH	

Cryptogram Quote

A	B	C	D	E	F	G	H	I	J	K	L	M
				T								

N	O	P	Q	R	S	T	U	V	W	X	Y	Z
				Y								

```
     E        E           R E                    R
 _ _     _ _ _    _ _ _ _ _ _ _      _ _ _
 Q H     I T      T R L Y T H H      X J Y

     R                  E,       E
 _ _ _ _ _ _ _ _ _ _    _ _    _ _ _ _
 C Y Q W B W J E T      I T    M J H W

   E     E R              R     E                        E
 _ _ _ _ _ _      _ _ _ _ _ _ _      _ _ _ _    _ _ _
 G T S T Y        D X Y C T W        W A Q W    W A T

               E                      R E
 _ _ _ _ _ _ _      _ _ _ _ _ _ _ _ _ _ _ _ _
 A B C A T H W      Q L L Y T V B Q W B X G

                                      E R          R
 _ _    _ _ _    _ _    _ _ _ _ _ _      _ _ _ _ _,
 B H    G X W    W X    J W W T Y        I X Y E H

                            E                    E
 _ _ _    _ _ _    _ _ _ _ _    _ _    _ _ _ _.
 U J W    W X      K B S T      U F    W A T M
```

— John F. Kennedy

Write about your ideal day:

Peaceful Piano

BSSA SIGNTR	☐☐☐☐ ☐☐☐☐☐☐
AMMHER	☐☐☐☐☐
OEYABKRD	☐☐☐☐☐☐☐
CMIUS ELSFH	☐☐☐☐ ☐☐☐☐☐
HETSE MSIUC	☐☐☐☐ ☐☐☐☐☐
LBREET ITNSGR	☐☐☐☐☐ ☐☐☐☐☐
NGNTUI NPI	☐☐☐☐☐ ☐☐☐
AEDLP	☐☐☐☐☐

Letter Circle

Cryptogram Quote

A	B	C	D	E	F	G	H	I	J	K	L	M

N	O	P	Q	R	S	T	U	V	W	X	Y	Z
M					C							

$\overline{Q}\ \overline{O}\ \overline{P}\ \overline{X}\ \overline{L}\ \overline{X}\ \overline{W}\ \overline{J}\ \overline{Z}\quad \overline{L}\ \overset{S}{\overline{C}}\quad \overline{X}\ \overline{B}\ \overline{Z}$

$\overset{S}{\overline{C}}\ \overline{L}\ \overline{Q}\ \overline{H}\quad \overline{M}\ \overset{O}{\overline{D}}\quad \overline{H}\ \overset{O}{\overline{M}}\ \overline{Y}\ \overline{K}\ \overline{Z}$

$\overset{S}{\overline{C}}\ \overset{O}{\overline{M}}\ \overline{W}\ \overline{K}\ \overset{S}{\overline{C}}.$

—Aesop

Beautiful Days

BALMY

BREEZY

BRIGHT

CALM

CLEAR

CLOUDLESS

GLOWING

GORGEOUS

LOVELY

RAY

SUNNY

SUNSHINE

WARM

Rhymes with Mind

BIEHND

IDNLDECE

DNIDE

GNIRD

ILEDN

DIESNG

EWHNID

WNEDI

Letter Circle

Cryptogram Quote

A	B	C	D	E	F	G	H	I	J	K	L	M
				W				B				

N	O	P	Q	R	S	T	U	V	W	X	Y	Z

```
 _ I _ _     _ I _     _ _     _ _ _ _ _ _ E _ _ _
 V L B C     B C       M       K D U H W R O P S

 _ _ _ .     _ I _     _ _ _ E _     _ _ E _ _ E _
 H M T       B         L M J W       U W J W R

 _ E E _ _   _ I _ _     _ _ _ E _     _ _ E _ _ _ E .
 C W W U     V L B C     D U W         I W O D R W
```

—Maya Angelou

Wide-open Windows

EZBREE

UTANRCI

SGASL

ERDAP

SNIGGIN

AEUTNR

CTIPEUR

ISLUNHGT

Letter Circle

Cryptogram Quote

A	B	C	D	E	F	G	H	I	J	K	L	M
			V									

N	O	P	Q	R	S	T	U	V	W	X	Y	Z
H												

```
        O              D
___ ___ ___ ___ ___ ___ ___ ___ ___ ___ ___   ___ ___ ___
 C   W   Q   P   H   E   F   B   V   M   L   P   M    O   T   B

     O   O   D                           O
___ ___ ___ ___     ___ ___ ___ ___   ___ ___ ___
 M   H   H   V       O   T   C   O     G   H   N

              D                                        O
___ ___ ___ ___ ___ ___   ___ ___ ___ ___   ___ ___   ___ ___ ___ ___
 C   F   I   B   C   V  G   T   C   X   B    L   P    G   H   N   I

       ___ ___ ___ ___   ___ ___   ___ ___ ___
        F   L   R   B     L   Z     O   T   B

     O           D           O               O
___ ___ ___ ___ ___ ___ ___ ___ ___ ___   ___ ___ ___   ___ ___ ___
 R   H   N   P   V   C   O   L   H   P     R   H   I     C   F   F

           D
___ ___ ___ ___ ___ ___ ___ ___ ___ ___.
 C   Y   N   P   V   C   P   W   B
```

—Eckhart Tolle

Think About It

BROOD	DELIBERATE	REFLECT
CHEW OVER	MEDITATE	REMEMBER
COGITATE	MULL OVER	REVIEW
CONCENTRATE	MUSE	RUMINATE
CONTEMPLATE	PONDER	SLEEP ON IT
	RECALL	

Mood-boosting Colors

BURTET EYOLLW

OTH INKP

NERF GNEER

REAGON

EEPD LUPERP

SCAATOL LBUE

NMTI EEGRN

ENSISRU GARENO

Letter Circle

Monthly Gratitude Reflections

List five things you're grateful for this month:

1. ____

2. ____

3. ____

4. ____

5. ____

Write about one experience you had this month that you're especially grateful for:

List some people in your life that made you feel loved this month:

List one big goal you'd like to accomplish this month:

____

____

____

____

What are some emotions you'd like to let go of this month?

-
-
-
-
-

What are some emotions you'd like to carry into this month?

-
-
-
-
-

Write some positive affirmations you can use throughout the month:

1. ____

2. ____

3. ____

Gratitude for Kids

ACTIVITIES	JAR	SHARE
CONCEPT	JOURNAL	SHOW
CULTIVATE	KINDNESS	TEACH
ENCOURAGE	LESSON	UNDERSTAND
ENGAGE	PRACTICE	

Rhymes with Peace

EASECR

CIYPEEEE

CEEFLE

EESGE

SREAGE

AESCERDE

EINCE

OLEICP

Letter Circle

Cryptogram Quote

A	B	C	D	E	F	G	H	I	J	K	L	M
O											C	

N	O	P	Q	R	S	T	U	V	W	X	Y	Z

L _ _ _   A   L _ _ _   _ _ L L   _ _
C U S T   O   C U A T   A G C C   L A

_ _ _ _ L _ _ _ ,   _ _ A _ _ _ _ _ ,
Z G W U C U Y I   B F O Y U Y G P T

_ _ _ _ L L _ _ _ A L _
U D Y T C C T J Y G O C

_ _ _ _ _ _ _ _ _ ,   A _ _   _ _ _ _ _
J G F U L X U Y I   O D P   D T S T F

_ _ _ _ L _ A _ _ _ _ .
X Y L N C T O F D U D B

— GZA

A vision board is a visual reminder of your goals and intentions. Inspire yourself and create a monthly vision board using this page to collage, doodle, sketch...or all of the above!

Places to Puzzle

OBREOMD

ABINC

FEOFCE BLATE

OLTHE

LSCHOO

BATLE

GTNIWAI ROMO

LOROF

Letter Circle

L E N
R Y E
E S

Be Still

CALM	QUIET	SUBDUED
FREE	RESTFUL	TRANQUIL
HARMONY	SERENE	UNDISTURBED
HUSH	SETTLE	UNRUFFLED
PEACEFUL	SILENCE	ZAZEN
	SIT CROSS-LEGGED	

Quiet Time

HDUESH

WLO GKIATLN

EMFDLUF

ULFESTR

RNUITLAQ

IREWPSH

PEESLCESHS

NISLECE

Letter Circle

What would you do if you won the lottery?

Tranquil Plants

OALE

BAOMOB

IOANSB

SMSO

PAEEC LYIL

OWLIWL ERET

TAERIWSI

AKSEN

Letter Circle

Cryptogram Quote

A	B	C	D	E	F	G	H	I	J	K	L	M
				R				J				

N	O	P	Q	R	S	T	U	V	W	X	Y	Z

```
      I     E  I        I   E .
V L D H J H P F R   J C   L J S I R C

        I        I        E .
S O Q B Z D J E H   J C   B O X R L H U
```

—Doris Day

Connect with Nature

BIRD-WATCH	COLLECT ROCKS	PICK FLOWERS
BOATING	FISH	RIVER RAFT
CAMP	FOSSILS	SHELLS
CANOE	HIKE	TAKE PHOTOS
CLIMB	KAYAKING	WALK
	LONG DRIVE	

Self-care Night

AHBT

IMETTEAD

THSRECT

EARD

NKSAC

ESPEL

EDDCLU

EMIVO

Letter Circle

N E
S   E
E M T T
T N
T I

Cryptogram Quote

A	B	C	D	E	F	G	H	I	J	K	L	M
A						T					H	

N	O	P	Q	R	S	T	U	V	W	X	Y	Z

    _L_   _ _ _   _ _   _ _ _   _A_
    G   H G N   G S   B N R   A M

    _ _G_ _ ,   _A_ _ _ _   _ _ _ _ _G
    S G T O M   A C M N I   N S R G S T

    _ _   _ _A_ _ _   _ _ _ _   _ _ _
    E K   L I A K N I F   Z G M O   M O N

    _ _ _ _ _ :   _ _A_ _   _ _ _ ,   _G_ _ ,
    Z D I R F   M O A S W   K D V   T D R

    _ _ _   _ALL_   _ _A_   _ _   _G_ _ _
    C D I   A H H   M O A M   G F   T D D R

    _A_   _ _ _   _A_   _A_   _ _ _ _ _ _ _ _ _L_ .
    A S R   R N A I   A S R   B N A V M G C V H

— Anne Frank

make
happiness
a habit

Peaceful Personalities

ODCTECLLE

NAROOHUSIM

TLRUEFS

ESENRE

OTOSHM

ITHOSNOG

AIRNQLTU

TOEHREUDBN

Letter Circle

Cryptogram Quote

A	B	C	D	E	F	G	H	I	J	K	L	M

N	O	P	Q	R	S	T	U	V	W	X	Y	Z
	F				N							

```
  O        O           O T     T
_____    _______    _______  _______
U M F    C F D O    R F N     N M A R T

  O          T T              O T
_____    _________   _______  _______
W F G    P E N N P D  U E P P  R F N

  T            O
_______    _______  _______ .
N M A R T   W F G    J K B M
```

—Estonian Proverb

Grateful Emotions

APPRECIATIVE	GRACIOUS	PLEASED
CALM	GRATIFIED	RELIEVED
CONTENT	HAPPY	SATISFIED
DELIGHTED	INDEBTED	THANKFUL
GLAD	PEACEFUL	THOUGHTFUL

Rhymes with Care

EBAR

IACRH

RLAIF

EARGL

ESCRA

SNERA

WRAE

RASEP

Letter Circle

List five things you're grateful for this month:

1. ____

2. ____

3. ____

4. ____

5. ____

Write about one experience you had this month that you're especially grateful for:

List some people in your life that made you feel loved this month:

List one big goal you'd like to accomplish this month:

____

____

____

____

What are some emotions you'd like to let go of this month?

-
-
-
-
-

What are some emotions you'd like to carry into this month?

-
-
-
-
-

Write some positive affirmations you can use throughout the month:

1. ____

2. ____

3. ____

Gratitude Garden

AFRICAN VIOLET	IRIS	PANSY
CAMELLIA	LAVENDER	PEONY
CAMPANULA	LILIES	PINK ROSE
CHRISTMAS CACTUS	MARANTA	PRIMROSE
HYDRANGEA	ORCHID	SWEET PEA

Cryptogram Quote

A	B	C	D	E	F	G	H	I	J	K	L	M
				i			s					

N	O	P	Q	R	S	T	U	V	W	X	Y	Z

```
  E       E         E
_ _   _ _ _ _ _ _   _ _ _ _ _
L I   E I D M O I B D A T Z F

              E
_ _ _ _ _ _ _ _ _   _ _ _
G M D F H F Z B I   D O B

  H           _   H
_ _ _ _ _ _ _ _   _ _ _   _ _
S Z J H E H F W   F S D F Y T

        E       E   H
_ _ _ _   _ _ _ _ _ _   _ _ _   _
J D O W   P I T P E I   S D B   D

H                     E
_ _ _ _   _ _   _ _ _   _ _ _ _ _ _ .
S D O B   H O   T Z M   Y Z C C I Y Y
```

—Michelle Obama

Meditation Vibes

TRAEEHB

LNATMEPETOC

MDARE

OEXRLEP

AMRNTA

RDOEPN

EPTSREN

TFLECRE

Letter Circle

Monthly Vision Board

A vision board is a visual reminder of your goals and intentions. Inspire yourself and create a monthly vision board using this page to collage, doodle, sketch...or all of the above!

Vacation Vibes

AIRPLANE	HOTEL	SAND
BEACH	PALM TREE	SUITCASE
COCKTAIL	PASSPORT	SUNGLASSES
GETAWAY	POOL	SUNSCREEN
HEAL	ROAD TRIP	TOWEL

Cryptogram Quote

A	B	C	D	E	F	G	H	I	J	K	L	M
F				I								

N	O	P	Q	R	S	T	U	V	W	X	Y	Z

```
      A                       E
 J Y  F  V N V U O I    S D D R H   V D

      E        A              A              E
 V G  I    K F H V    F  L O    S D P I   V D

      E              E   E   ;       E A
 V G  I    K Y I H I L V     A I F Y

    A   A              E ,              ,    A
 F P F Y N W I     S U H V     F L O

 A                                 A   E A
 F X E N V N D L    S D D R    F G I F O
```

— C. S. Lewis

Grateful Spirit

EITADTUT

EESNSEC

ITTEYIDN

IENDTMS

PTVESEEPRIC

ULSO

EBING

FILEEB

Letter Circle

Gratitude

ACKNOWLEDGE
APPRECIATE
BLESSING
CREDIT
ENJOY

GRACE
GRATEFUL
INDEBTED
OBLIGED
PRAISE
RECOGNITION

RELISH
SAVOR
THANKS
THANKSGIVING
TRIBUTE

Where do you see yourself in one year? Five years? Ten years?

Watch the Sunrise

ALTKEBN

CFEFEO

AMECRA

EDYAARBK

IEVW

SLAUSSNGES

ICNICP

OMRHSTE

Letter Circle

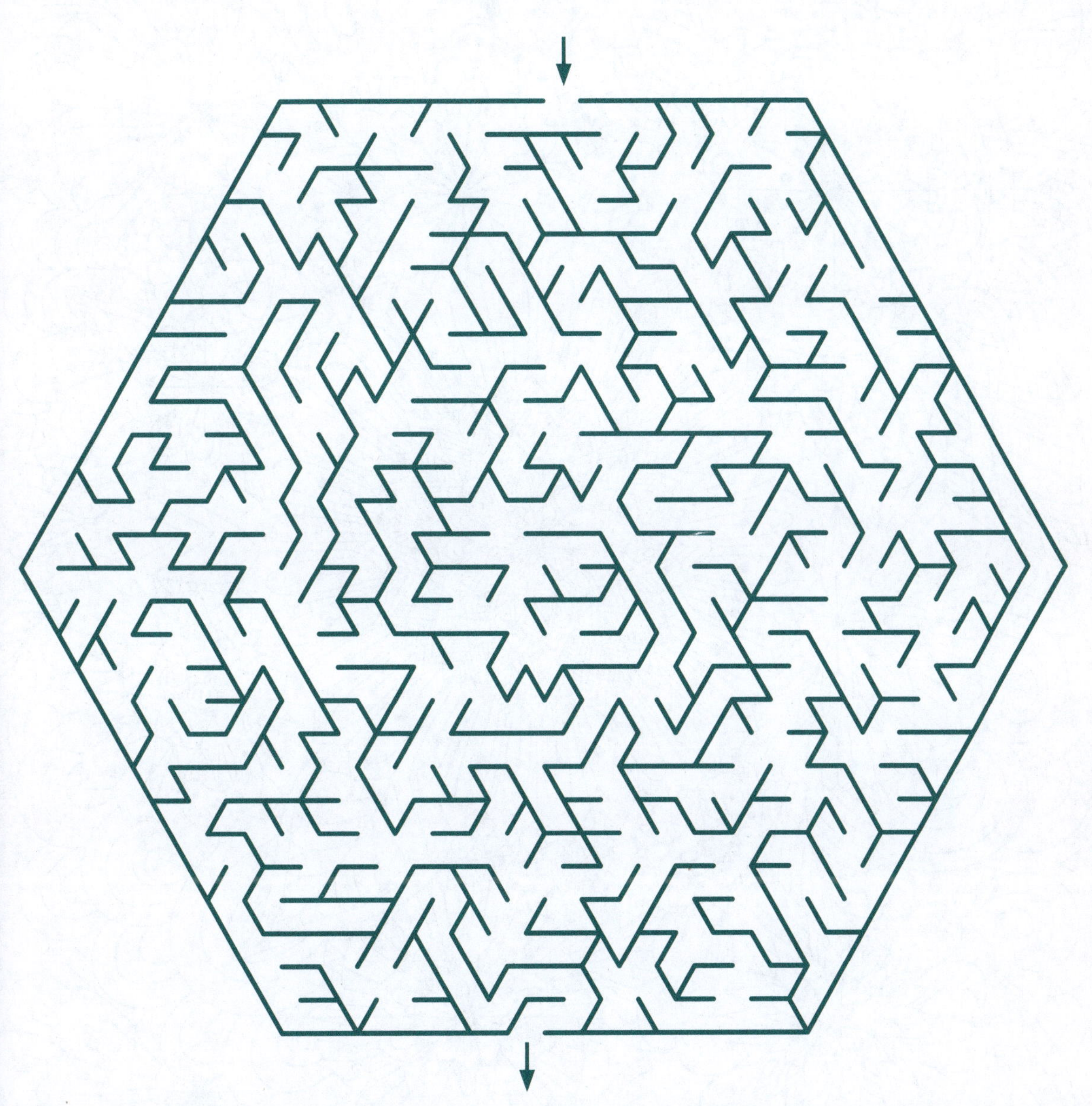

Breathwork

AONMAILBD

YLELB

NCOUT

DPEE EAHTRB

XIEECRES

CUFSO

SRONLTI

DPAMRHGIA

Letter Circle

Dream Words

BUBBLE	FANTASY	PICTURE
CHIMERA	HALLUCINATE	PIPE DREAM
DAYDREAM	IDEA	THOUGHT
DELUSION	IMAGE	TRANCE
DREAM CATCHER	IMAGINATION	TRIP
	NIGHTMARE	

Cryptogram Quote

A	B	C	D	E	F	G	H	I	J	K	L	M
											T	

N	O	P	Q	R	S	T	U	V	W	X	Y	Z
C												

```
 ’__    ___L_L    ___N____N
 B O    H Z B T T    Z E D C V B C L

 _L_L    ___    ______,    __N_
 D T T    Z E G    H Z D M H    U C G

 __    __N_.
 A N    U C G
```

—Marissa Meyer

Intentions for Spring

NAENDCUBA

AHECNG

SNCEELA

RETURUN

RBRHETI

RHREFES

ECMEOWL

PATLN

Letter Circle

143

Mindfulness Types

YBDO NSCA

EAHBTIRNG

ARTMNA

MNIAETOTDI

EMVTOMNE

CSRTTEH

TOSILNIAAIUZV

YGAO

Letter Circle

Thankful in Other Languages

AGRADECIDO	GRATI	SHAKIRIN
BLAGODARNYY	HÁLÁS	TACKSAM
DANKBAR	KHOBCHAI	TAKNEMMELIG
GODIYA	MAHADSANID	ZAHVALAN

Cryptogram Quote

A	B	C	D	E	F	G	H	I	J	K	L	M
				B								

N	O	P	Q	R	S	T	U	V	W	X	Y	Z
							L					

```
_ _ _   _ _E,  _E _ _E   _ _ _U _E
I V P   R B   B Q B P O   U V L N B

_ _   _ _ _ _E.   _ _ _   _   _E _E _
W N   Z P X M B   X E S   W   I B B K

_ _ _ _U_E_E   _ _   _ _   _E _ _ _
Z P X C W C L S B   W E   R O   U B X P C

E_ _ _   _ _E_   _   _ _E   _E _E _
B X M U   C W R B   W   M X E   R B B C

_ _ _E_ _E_   _ _ _   _ _ _ _   _ _
N V R B V E B   X E S   K V V F   X C

_ _ _   _ _   _ _E _   _ _ _ _E_.
U W N   V P   U B P   N R W K B
```

—Elie Wiesel

Monthly Gratitude Reflections

List five things you're grateful for this month:

1. ____

2. ____

3. ____

4. ____

5. ____

Write about one experience
you had this month that you're
especially grateful for:

List some people in your life that
made you feel loved this month:

Monthly Plans and Goals

List one big goal you'd like to accomplish this month:

____

____

____

____

What are some emotions you'd like to let go of this month?

-
-
-
-
-

What are some emotions you'd like to carry into this month?

-
-
-
-
-

Write some positive affirmations you can use throughout the month:

1. ____

2. ____

3. ____

Grateful Animals

SGDO

CNEMPZEHIA

YTRKUE

IMAPLA

REIVPMA ABT

CSAT

IHONLDP

ELEANPHT

Letter Circle

Visualization Practice

ACHIEVE

AMBITIONS

DREAMS

END GOAL

FUTURE

HEAR

IMAGINE

PRACTICE

RELAXED

SENSES

SIGHT

SMELL

SUBCONSCIOUS

TASTE

TECHNIQUE

TOUCH

A vision board is a visual reminder of your goals and intentions. Inspire yourself and create a monthly vision board using this page to collage, doodle, sketch...or all of the above!

Rhymes with Love

VEDO

HFOREE

YOALELDV

ESHOV

HTFOERE

BAEVO

ELOGV

ORTS FO

Letter Circle

Cryptogram Quote

A	B	C	D	E	F	G	H	I	J	K	L	M
						X						

N	O	P	Q	R	S	T	U	V	W	X	Y	Z
	B											

```
_ O       _ _ _ _     _ _     _ O _ _
G B       V N I Q     L P     O B D M

_ _ G _ _ _     _ _ _ _     G _ _ _ _ G
N D X M G I     I W S G     X L Z L G X

        _ _ _ _ _ _ .
        I W S G T P
```

— James Allen

Authors of Gratitude

ARRIEN	FOLEY	SACKS
BROWN	JACOBS	SAFFRIN
DEMOSS	KRALIK	SPINELLI
DEPAOLA	MARKES	WILLEMS
EMMONS	MORA	

Cryptogram Quote

A	B	C	D	E	F	G	H	I	J	K	L	M

N	O	P	Q	R	S	T	U	V	W	X	Y	Z
						N					T	

```
    Y       T          T T
_ _ _ _ _   _ _ _   _ _ _ _ _
S L U G T   N H S   C J N N C S

T                             Y
_ _ _ _ _ _ ,  _ _ _   _ _ _  _ _ _
N H J L Z W    X G I   G L S  F A T

  Y           Y
_ _ _   _ _ _   _ _ _ _   _ _ _ _
T G M   B A T   C G G P   V A D P

                        T       Y
_ _ _   _ _ _ _ _ _ _   _ _ _ _
A L F   I S A C J Y S   N H S T

          T                 T
_ _ _ _   _ _ _   _ _ _   _ _ _ _ _ _ .
O S I S   N H S   V J Z   N H J L Z W
```

—Robert Brault

Who are the most influential and inspiring people in your life?

Faith Words

ILEVBEE

OVINOETD

OHEP

VOEL

CENARLEI

UTRTS

OWRPSIH

PRSOSFE

Letter Circle

Types of Worship

APPRECIATION

BIBLE

INFORMAL

LEARNING

LITURGICAL

MEDITATE

MUSICAL

NONLITURGICAL

OBSERVE

PRAYER

PRIVATE

READING

SERVICE

SINGING

TEACH

TESTIMONY

Cryptogram Quote

A	B	C	D	E	F	G	H	I	J	K	L	M
				J	O							

N	O	P	Q	R	S	T	U	V	W	X	Y	Z

```
_ E   _ _ _ _   _ F _ _   _ _ _ E   _ _
M J    K F S E    O U B G    E U K J    E D

_ _ _ _   _ _ _   _ _ _ _   _ _ E
S E D L    P B G    E Q P B C    E Q J

_ E _ _ E _   _ _ _   _ _ E _   _
L J D L Z J    M Q D    K P C J    P

_ _ F F E _ E _ _ E _   _ _   _ _ _
G U O O J Y J B H J    U B    D F Y

_ _ E _ _ .
Z U A J S
```

— John F. Kennedy

Cryptogram Quote

A	B	C	D	E	F	G	H	I	J	K	L	M
			T				X					

N	O	P	Q	R	S	T	U	V	W	X	Y	Z
					U							

```
_ _ _ _ _D    _ _ _ _ _ _ _    _H_ _
I  W N M Z T  R S I P C S I P   C X S C

_H_ _ _ _S    _ _ _    _H_ _    _H_ _H_ _S
C X S P V U   S B A    C X A    X I Y X A U C

_ _ _ _   _ _   _H_ _ _H_;   _ _D
H N B R   N H   C X N M Y X C   S P T

_H_ _   _ _ _ _ _ _D_   _S
C X S C   Y B S C I C M T A   I U

H_ _ _ _ _ _S_S    _D_ _ _ _ _D_   _ _
X S L L I P A U U   T N M J Z A T   J O

_ _ _D_ _ _.
W N P T A B
```

—G. K. Chesterton

Night Sky

TRASYR

HTGITIWL

NALGITFLH

VESANEH

SDKU

EICLTEASL

RULAN

YKNI

Letter Circle

Gratitude Symbols

AUTUMN	CORNUCOPIA	HUMMINGBIRD
BOWING	DOLPHIN	PROSTRATION
BUFFALO	FISH HOOK	ROSE
CHRYSANTHEMUM	GIFTS	SPIRAL
CIRCLE	HANDSHAKE	SWEET PEAS

Stress Relief

NUUPCTRUCAE

BEATEHR

COCTNNE

ENNSCIUOGL

HLGAU

ESAGSAM

MIUSC

TREYPHA

Letter Circle

Monthly Gratitude Reflections

List five things you're grateful for this month:

1. ____

2. ____

3. ____

4. ____

5. ____

Write about one experience you had this month that you're especially grateful for:

List some people in your life that made you feel loved this month:

Monthly Plans and Goals

List one big goal you'd like to accomplish this month:

____

____

____

____

What are some emotions you'd like to let go of this month?

-
-
-
-
-

What are some emotions you'd like to carry into this month?

-
-
-
-
-

Write some positive affirmations you can use throughout the month:

1. ____

2. ____

3. ____

Count Your Blessings

CLOTHES

EDUCATION

EXPERIENCES

FAMILY

FOOD

FREEDOM

FRIENDS

GOD

HEALTH

HOUSE

JOB

LOVE

MONEY

PETS

SAFETY

SECURITY

Deep Conversation

ERATBN

IHHATCCT

OVEENCSR

EIATEBRDLE

SUECIRDOS

CEGHANXE

ELALVBRNEU

HAERS

Letter Circle

Cryptogram Quote

A	B	C	D	E	F	G	H	I	J	K	L	M
E												

N	O	P	Q	R	S	T	U	V	W	X	Y	Z
X	R											

```
___ ___      ___ ___ ___ ___ ___ ___      ___ ___ A__ ___ ___ N__
 I   L   D    U   D   D   N   D   S   I    K   A   E   H   W   X   F

O__ ___      ___ ___ A__ N__      N__ A__ ___ ___ ___ ___      ___ ___
 R   J        L   G   B   E   X    X   E   I   G   A   D        W   S

___ ___ ___      N__ ___ ___ ___      ___ ___      O__ ___
 I   L   D        X   D   D   U        I   R        Z   D

A__ ___ ___ ___ ___ ___ ___ ___ A__ ___ ___ ___.
 E   N   N   A   D   K   W   E   I   D   U
```

— William James

Monthly Vision Board

A vision board is a visual reminder of your goals and intentions. Inspire yourself and create a monthly vision board using this page to collage, doodle, sketch...or all of the above!

Peaceful Animals

TRBEYTLUF

NECAR

OEVD

OSRHE

SINEHIFGRK

NAMEAET

APDAN

OSTLH

Letter Circle

K
N S
N S E
I D

Vision Board

COLLAGE	DREAM	PHYSICAL
CORKBOARD	GLUE	POSTER
CREATE	GOAL	UPCOMING
CUT	MAGAZINE	WORDS
DIGITAL	MANIFEST	
	PHOTO	

Cryptogram Quote

A	B	C	D	E	F	G	H	I	J	K	L	M
H			V									

N	O	P	Q	R	S	T	U	V	W	X	Y	Z
									N			

W_ ____ _ __A___D
N B Q J   L   Z G H U G Q V

_______ __
E Y D J G L J X   M I

_________, __ _W___
A R Q Z Z L J X Z   M I   N B Y R Q

_____ _____D _A___D.
R L T Q   G D U J Q V   H U Y D J V

— Willie Nelson

Write ten things that make you the most happy in life.

Intentions for Winter

ULFYOJ

ACML

TMOCIM

EONTCCN

NIEZOSCS

AEUNSRTNDD

TFELRCE

LEAH

Letter Circle

E I B S S G L N

Cryptogram Quote

A	B	C	D	E	F	G	H	I	J	K	L	M
				O								

N	O	P	Q	R	S	T	U	V	W	X	Y	Z
									R			

```
_ _ _ _ _ _ _ E _      _ E _ _ _ W _
H S A K W K U J O      E O B K X R B

_ E _ E _ E _ E_     _ _ _ _ _ _ _ _
S O F O S O L D O     D P A L H W L H

_ _ _ E _ E _      _ _ W _ WE
N X S O F O S      P X R   R O

E _ E _ _ E _ E _      _ _ _ E _ _ _
O Z G O S W O L D O    I W N O   A L J

_ _ E _ W _ _ _ _ _.
K P O   R X S I J
```

— John Milton

Effects of Gratitude

BRAIN HEALTH	MOOD	SELF-ESTEEM
DOPAMINE	PHYSICALITY	SEROTONIN
EMOTIONS	POSITIVITY	SLEEP
HEALTH	RELATIONSHIPS	WILLPOWER
IMMUNITY	SELF-CARE	

Cuddle Up

WSDLDEA

EHWITDGE NLTKBAE

OOTRERFMC

ABYB

ANGTEIH DPA

TNERRAP

LISGPENE BGA

FTUSFDE ALNAMI

Letter Circle

Cryptogram Quote

A	B	C	D	E	F	G	H	I	J	K	L	M
M												

N	O	P	Q	R	S	T	U	V	W	X	Y	Z
						Z						

A _ A _ _ A _ _ A
M R O M V C   A M L K   M Q

A T T _ T _ _ _ _ _
M Z Z J Z H T K   X W

_ _ A T _ T _ _ _ _ _.
D I M Z J Z H T K

—Sterling K. Brown

Get Outside

RHCABIW-TD

IPEEENBGEK

AENRDG

GORAOPHHPT

OPIOKNCLORG

RAGATSZE

NHGIIK

NIPICC

Letter Circle

____

____

____

_________________ _________________

_________________ _________________

Cryptogram Quote

A	B	C	D	E	F	G	H	I	J	K	L	M
				U								

N	O	P	Q	R	S	T	U	V	W	X	Y	Z
Q												

$$\frac{}{C}\frac{E}{U}\frac{}{T}\frac{}{R} \quad \frac{}{P}\frac{N}{Q}\frac{}{D} \quad \frac{}{W}\frac{E}{U}$$

$$\frac{}{R}\frac{}{I}\frac{}{P}\frac{N}{Q}\frac{}{G}\frac{}{B}\frac{}{E}\frac{}{Z}.$$

— William Wordsworth

Places to Find Joy

BEACH   LIBRARY   TEMPLE

CHURCH   MOSQUE   THEATER

GARDEN   PARK   VACATION

HOME   RESTAURANT   WITH FAMILY

KITCHEN   SCHOOL   YOGA STUDIO

               STORE

Rhymes with Calm

AUQLM

MAPLS

MEMALB

LMIAS

MBBO

BAML

PORM

LAPM

Letter Circle

Monthly Gratitude Reflections

List five things you're grateful for this month:

1. ____

2. ____

3. ____

4. ____

5. ____

Write about one experience you had this month that you're especially grateful for:

List some people in your life that made you feel loved this month:

 # Monthly Plans and Goals 

List one big goal you'd like to accomplish this month:

____

____

____

____

What are some emotions you'd like to let go of this month?

-
-
-
-
-

What are some emotions you'd like to carry into this month?

-
-
-
-
-

Write some positive affirmations you can use throughout the month:

1. ____

2. ____

3. ____

Keep a Calm Home

CENLDA

COLRO

ORTAAAYREPHM

EPNO IWWODN

RDETETLCU

ODGO WOFL

TLINGGHI

HSONTOGI SODUNS

Letter Circle

Family Traditions

BIRTHDAYS	GIFTS	PHOTOS
CAR RIDES	HOLIDAYS	PICNIC
CRAFTING	MOVIE NIGHT	RESTAURANT
FOOD	MUSEUM	VACATION
GAMES	PARK	

Monthly Vision Board

A vision board is a visual reminder of your goals and intentions. Inspire yourself and create a monthly vision board using this page to collage, doodle, sketch...or all of the above!

Happy Words

RPIHYC

LEEG

LLOJY

EPPYP

SNNGHII

MSRMEUY

ISKNPRGAL

KCLTDIE

Letter Circle

Focus
on the
Good

Cryptogram Quote

A	B	C	D	E	F	G	H	I	J	K	L	M
					A							

N	O	P	Q	R	S	T	U	V	W	X	Y	Z
O		I										

```
__ __ __ __ __ __ __ __ __   __ __   __
K  M  Y  S  J  S  E  B  U    J  C    Y

P                  F
__ __ __ __ __ __ __   __ __ __ __ __ __ __
I  F  Q  U  M  A  E    W  Y  S  Y  T  R  C  S

F              P  P  N              '
__ __ __   __ __ __ __ __ __ __ .  __ __ __
A  F  M    P  Y  I  I  J  O  U  C    J  S  C

          P
__ __ __   __ __ __ __ __   __ __ __ __   __ __ __ __ __ __
S  P  U    C  I  Y  M  Z    S  P  Y  S    T  J  K  P  S  C

     F                 F              N
__   __ __ __ __   __ __   __ __ __   __ __
Y    A  J  M  U    F  A    H  F  R    J  O

__ __ __ __   __ __ __ __ .
R  F  E  M    C  F  E  T
```

—Amy Collette

Acts of Kindness

BAKE	FEED BIRDS	SEND A CARD
COMPLIMENT	GIFT	TAKE CARE
CONVERSE	GIVE	TELL A JOKE
DO A CHORE	HOLD THE DOOR	THANK YOU
DONATE	PAY IT FORWARD	VOLUNTEER
	REUSE	

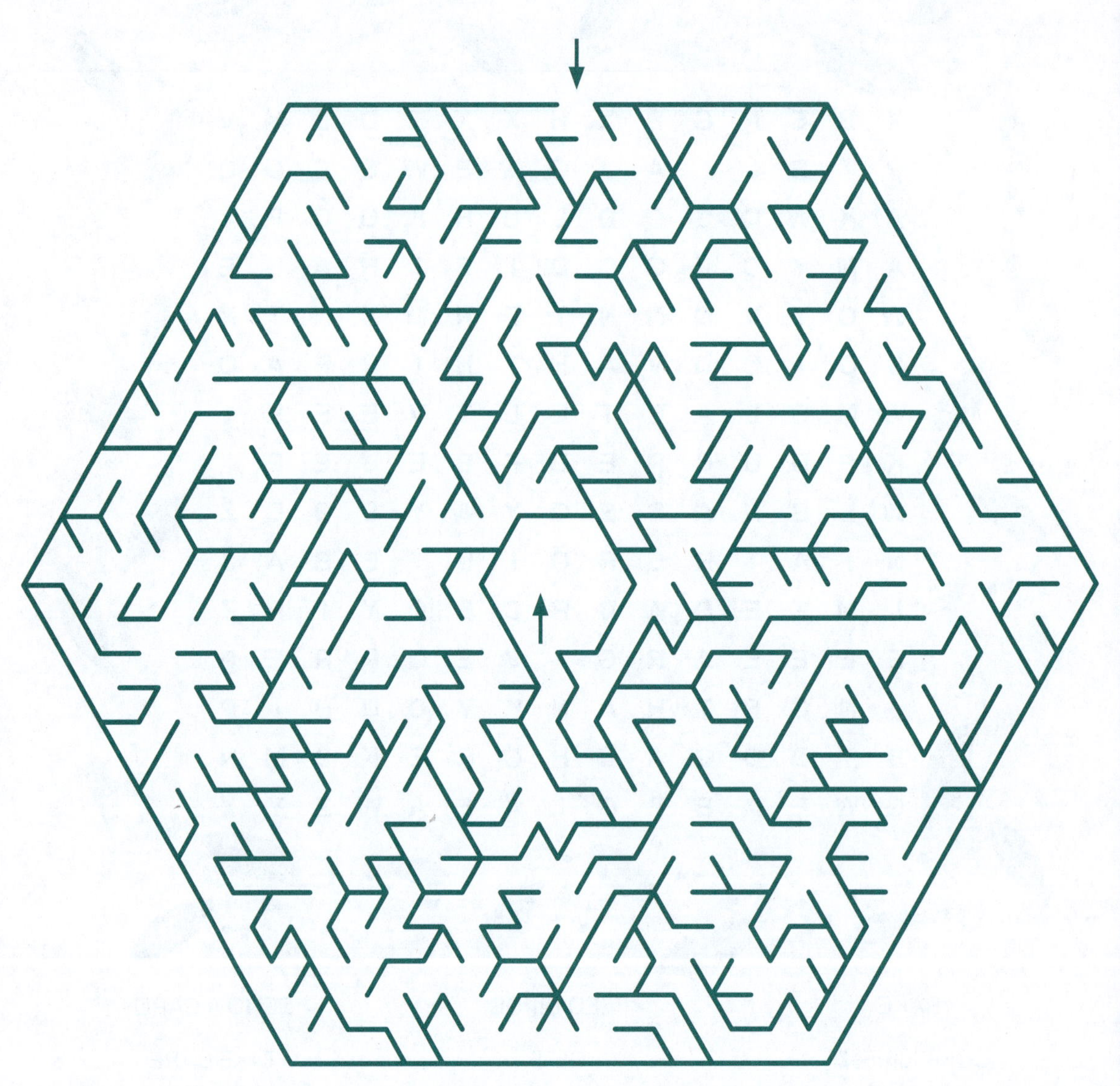

Cryptogram Quote

<table>
<tr><td>A</td><td>B</td><td>C</td><td>D</td><td>E</td><td>F</td><td>G</td><td>H</td><td>I</td><td>J</td><td>K</td><td>L</td><td>M</td></tr>
<tr><td></td><td></td><td></td><td></td><td></td><td></td><td></td><td></td><td></td><td></td><td></td><td>V</td><td></td></tr>
<tr><td>N</td><td>O</td><td>P</td><td>Q</td><td>R</td><td>S</td><td>T</td><td>U</td><td>V</td><td>W</td><td>X</td><td>Y</td><td>Z</td></tr>
<tr><td></td><td></td><td>W</td><td></td><td></td><td>P</td><td></td><td></td><td></td><td></td><td></td><td></td><td></td></tr>
</table>

L ___ ___   S ___   ___ ___   ___ ___ ___ ___ ___ ___ L ___   ___ ___
V O N   Y P   G O   Z J F N O R Y V   N X

___ ___ ___   P ___ ___ P L ___   ___ ___ ___   ___ ___ ___
N M O   W O X W V O   L M X   U F B O

___ S ___   ___ ___ P P P ___ ;   ___ ___ ___ ___   ___ ___ ___   ___ ___ ___
Y P   M F W W D   N M O D   F J O   N M O

___ ___ ___ ___ ___ ___ ___ ___   ___ ___ ___ ___ ___ ___ ___ ___ S ___
K M F J U A C Z   Z F J I O C O J P

___ ___ ___   ___ ___ ___ ___   ___ ___ ___   ___ S ___   ___ L S ___
L M X   U F B O   X Y J   P X Y V P

___ L ___ S ___ S ___ ___ ___.
G V X P P X U

— Marcel Proust

Which foods nourish your soul the most and why?

Glass Half Full

CHERYE

ETAECVRI

ECTNREEIG

PHAYP

FPUHOLE

MSTNIED

IPSTMOMI

EPOSIIVT

Letter Circle

N
S   A
U
M   G
I

Powerful Gratitude

CAPABLE	IMPORTANT	POTENT
CELEBRATED	INFLUENTIAL	PROMINENT
EFFECTIVE	MEANINGFUL	SIGNIFICANT
EFFICIENT	MIGHTY	STRONG
GREAT	NOTABLE	

Cryptogram Quote

A	B	C	D	E	F	G	H	I	J	K	L	M
				B								

N	O	P	Q	R	S	T	U	V	W	X	Y	Z
				G		H						

```
_ E _   _ _ _   _ _ _ _   _ E _   _ _ _ _
I B     A V P   K P M U   Z B     T V C W

_ _   _ E _   _ _ _ _ _   _ _   _ _ _ _ E
H K   Z B     V M C J B   C P   H F K T B

_ _ E _ T _ _   _ _ E _   _ _ R
Q K Q B P H T   I F B P   K N G

_ E _ R T _   _ R E _   _ _ _ _ _ _ _ _
F B V G H T   V G B     A K P T A C K N T

_ _   _ _ R   T R E _   _ R E _ _ _ _ _ .
K O   K N G   H G B V   T N G B T
```

—Thornton Wilder

Cryptogram Quote

A	B	C	D	E	F	G	H	I	J	K	L	M
												O

N	O	P	Q	R	S	T	U	V	W	X	Y	Z
					R							

```
 _  _  _      _  _      _  _  _  _  _  _  _  _  _ S,   _  _  _
 X  M  T      L  M      F  Y  C  F  K  D  M  M  K  R   X  M  T

 _  _      _  _  _  _  _ S,   _ S _  _  _      _ '_      _  _  _  _
 L  M      D  A  L  K  R      R  T  I  V  V    I  J      V  I  K  C

 _  _      _  _  _  _  _ S _ S   _ M _      _  _  _  _  _ S.
 T  M      C  W  E  U  C  R  R   O  B       T  Y  A  L  K  R

 _      _  _  _      _  _  _ S   _  _  _      _  _      _  _  _
 I      X  M  T      T  Y  C  R  P  L        I  L      T  Y  C

 M _  _  _  _  _  _      _  _  _      M _  _  _
 O  M  U  L  I  L  X     A  L  J      O  M  M  L  T  Y  C

 _  _      _  _  _  _  _  _.
 A  T      L  I  X  Y  T
```

Grounding

NIOTNNCOEC

HAECGR

HAETR

IOUFONDTNA

NADL

CCATEPRI

TNDSA

LSIO

Letter Circle

Y
H · L
A
P · P
I

Makes You Feel Warm and Fuzzy

BATH

BLANKET

BOOK

CAMPFIRE

COOKIES

GIFT

HANDHOLDING

HUG

LOVE LETTER

MUG

PET

ROBE

SNUGGLE

SOFT SOCKS

SOUP

STUFFED ANIMAL

Mood-boosting Herbs

ADORLHIO

HLYO AIBSL

CCLREIOI

NGENSIG

LOMNE LMBA

WDSAAGANAHH

ORES

NOMCINAN

Letter Circle

Monthly Gratitude Reflections

List five things you're grateful for this month:

1. ____

2. ____

3. ____

4. ____

5. ____

<table>
<tr>
<td>

Write about one experience you had this month that you're especially grateful for:

</td>
<td>

List some people in your life that made you feel loved this month:

</td>
</tr>
</table>

Monthly Plans and Goals

List one big goal you'd like to accomplish this month:

____

____

____

____

<table>
<tr><td>

What are some emotions you'd like to let go of this month?

-
-
-
-
-

</td><td>

What are some emotions you'd like to carry into this month?

-
-
-
-
-

</td></tr>
</table>

Write some positive affirmations you can use throughout the month:

1. ____

2. ____

3. ____

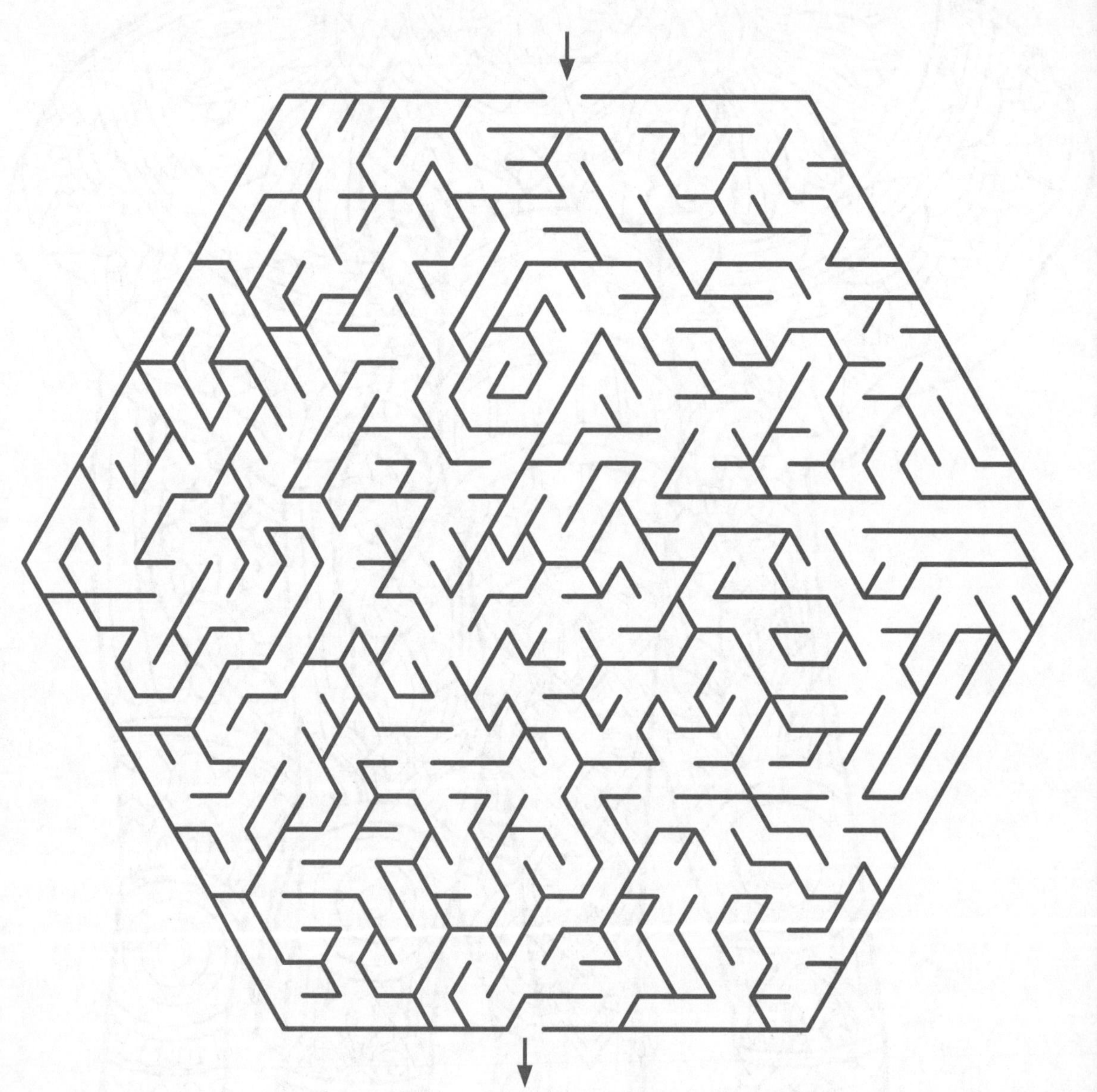

Breakfast in Bed

CABON

EABLG

EFCFEO

HECRNF TTAOS

ATTRAIFT

TOATS

MAALOET

OECNS

Letter Circle

Bath Essentials

CDYAD

EDLNAC

FSRUIEFD

URBBRE DCKU

WOLTE

NWEI

HSHATLWOC

PSA WOLPLI

Letter Circle

Monthly Vision Board

A vision board is a visual reminder of your goals and intentions. Inspire yourself and create a monthly vision board using this page to collage, doodle, sketch...or all of the above!

Work-life Balance

BREAK	IMPORTANCE	PRIORITIZE
DEMANDS	JOB	QUALITY
EMBRACE	LIFE	SELF-CARE
ENJOY	PERSONAL	TIME
HOURS	PLAN AHEAD	

Cryptogram Quote

<table>
<tr><td>A</td><td>B</td><td>C</td><td>D</td><td>E</td><td>F</td><td>G</td><td>H</td><td>I</td><td>J</td><td>K</td><td>L</td><td>M</td></tr>
<tr><td></td><td></td><td></td><td></td><td></td><td></td><td></td><td></td><td>U</td><td></td><td></td><td></td><td></td></tr>
<tr><td>N</td><td>O</td><td>P</td><td>Q</td><td>R</td><td>S</td><td>T</td><td>U</td><td>V</td><td>W</td><td>X</td><td>Y</td><td>Z</td></tr>
<tr><td></td><td></td><td></td><td></td><td></td><td>V</td><td></td><td></td><td></td><td></td><td></td><td></td><td></td></tr>
</table>

```
           I  S            S  I                    S
___        __            ___         __________
C  E  O    U  V    J  P  I    V  U  L  Y  F  I  V  J

                              I
____    __    __________________.
D  E  K  L    E  D    A  K  B  J  U  J  N  H  I
```

— Karl Barth

#Goals

RREACE

UIACDEATNOL

AMLYFI

NCAIAFLIN

SFNESTI

HTHEAL

OPRSLAEN

EOHNPARISILT

Letter Circle

Heart Center

ANAHATA   FORGIVENESS   PROFOUND

CHAKRA   FOURTH   RELATIONSHIP

CHEST   INTEGRATION   SELF-LOVE

COMPASSION   JOY   TRUTH

EMPATHY   LOVE   UNHURT

POINT

What are your favorite parts of yourself, the ones you're most grateful for?

Cryptogram Quote

A	B	C	D	E	F	G	H	I	J	K	L	M
								E				

N	O	P	Q	R	S	T	U	V	W	X	Y	Z
									B			

W _ _ _   W _ _   _ _ _ _ _   _ _   _ _ _
B G Y J   B Y   W O T F D   O J   O F Z

        I
_ _ _ _ _ _ _ _ _ ,   _ _ _   _ _ _ _
V Z R H E H F K Y   H G Y   H E K Y

    I   I
_ _   _ _ _ _ _ _ _ _ _ _ _ _ _
O W   K E D R C C O E J H L Y J H

                     I
_ _ _ _   _ _ _   _ _ _   _ _ _   _ _ _ _
V O Y D   O F H   R J K   H G Y   H E K Y

_ _   _ _ _ _   _ _ _ _ _   _ _ .
O W   M O S Y   Z F D G Y D   E J

—Kristin Armstrong

Nourishing Food

BEANS	GARLIC	SOY
BERRIES	KALE	SQUASH
FISH	LENTILS	WHOLE GRAINS
FLAXSEED	NUTS	YOGURT
	SEAWEED	

Mindful Puzzles

GRAMNAA

CROODSWRS

ORGCMTRPYA

WJGSIA

GIOCL

EAMZ

ILDDRE

DROW ARSHCE

Letter Circle

Good Friends

DEPENDABLE	INTEGRITY	PLAYFUL
EMPATHETIC	KIND	PROTECTIVE
ENCOURAGING	LOVING	THOUGHTFUL
GOOD LISTENER	LOYAL	TRUSTWORTHY
HONEST	NURTURING	YOU

Cryptogram Quote

A	B	C	D	E	F	G	H	I	J	K	L	M
				U								

N	O	P	Q	R	S	T	U	V	W	X	Y	Z
						Z						

```
      E           T              E             T                E
 R Y U Q   G Z   X F J U D     Z F      S G N U

 T   E            T              T
 Z Y U   X E G Z G X B S     Z Y G Q H     G D

         E T     E               T     E
     R Y U Z Y U E     A F L     Z B M U

 T                                      T E
 Z Y G Q H D   N F E   H E B Q Z U W   F E

     T       E       T     E           T
     Z B M U     Z Y U J     R G Z Y

         T     T       E.
 H E B Z G Z L W U              —G. K. Chesterton
```

233

Moon Ritual

GEIOFNRF

RNOC

IEMFENIN NEGYRE

LFUL NOMO

DEDSGSO

RSIHPWO

RLAEESE

EVSRATH

Letter Circle

Body Scan

NTHGISI

ESELAER

CSE-AFNOOMPLISS

UIEDDG

NENTSOI

NOTASENSI

ANOITMDTEI

Letter Circle

Manifestation

ALIGN	ENERGY	TRUST
ASK	FATHOM	UNIVERSE
ATTRACT	HIGHEST SELF	VIBRATION
DESIRE	INSPIRATION	VISION
EMOTION	REMOVE DOUBT	WILL
	SEEK	

Cryptogram Quote

A	B	C	D	E	F	G	H	I	J	K	L	M
											C	

N	O	P	Q	R	S	T	U	V	W	X	Y	Z
P												

```
          L                               L    N
 __  __ __ __ __    __ __ __ __    __ __ __ __ __    __ __
 E   C  E  Q  M      V  Y  G  V     C  T  P  M  K     S  T

 L                 L       N
 __ __ __ __,  __ __ __ __    __ __   __    __ __ __ __ __
 C  H  X  T     C  T  P  M     S  T    G     Y  T  G  Q  V

                     L
              __ __ __ __ __ __    __ __ __ __
              Q  T  I  C  T  V  T    N  H  V  Y

                 N                   L  N
        __ __ __ __ __ __ __ __ __ __ __ __.
        V  Y  G  P  U  X  Z  C  P  T  K  K
```

— William Shakespeare

Monthly Gratitude Reflections

List five things you're grateful for this month:

1. ____

2. ____

3. ____

4. ____

5. ____

Write about one experience you had this month that you're especially grateful for:

List some people in your life that made you feel loved this month:

Monthly Plans and Goals

List one big goal you'd like to accomplish this month:

____

____

____

____

What are some emotions you'd like to let go of this month?

-
-
-
-
-

What are some emotions you'd like to carry into this month?

-
-
-
-
-

Write some positive affirmations you can use throughout the month:

1. ____

2. ____

3. ____

Loving Kindness

MIATY

AHNCT

CSSOAIONMP

BDEMOY

OODG LWLI

IEEATMTD

RILDACA

BSLEIUM ATTES

Letter Circle

Home Life

COMFORT	GENERATIONS	REFUGE
ENTERTAINING	LODGING	RELIEF
FAMILY	NAP	REST
FOUNDATION	PETS	SHELTER
FRIENDS	PRIVATE	SOLACE

Monthly Vision Board

A vision board is a visual reminder of your goals and intentions. Inspire yourself and create a monthly vision board using this page to collage, doodle, sketch...or all of the above!

Energy Balancing

ODBCEKL ⬚⬚⬚⬚⬚⬚⬚

RNSECTE ⬚⬚⬚⬚⬚⬚⬚

RHAKCA ⬚⬚⬚⬚⬚⬚

DEXNPE ⬚⬚⬚⬚⬚⬚

HGEIANL ⬚⬚⬚⬚⬚⬚⬚

THRTNSGE ⬚⬚⬚⬚⬚⬚⬚⬚

ASETT ⬚⬚⬚⬚⬚

KNATIE ⬚⬚⬚⬚⬚⬚

Letter Circle

Cryptogram Quote

A	B	C	D	E	F	G	H	I	J	K	L	M
Y				O								

N	O	P	Q	R	S	T	U	V	W	X	Y	Z

```
  E                    A              E A
_ _ _   _ _ _ _ _ _ _ _ _   _ _ _ _
Q D O   S C Q D Y C A P S B   D O Y R Q

            E            E      E ;
_ _ _ _ _ _ _ _   _ _   _ _ _ _ _
G Z I L K V O R I   C K   X O R L Z O I

      E          A              E A
_ _ _   _ _ _   _ _ _ _ _ _ _ _ _   _ _ _ _
E S Q   Q D O   Q D Y C A P S B   D O Y R Q

                        E   E
_ _ _ _   _ _ _ _ ,   _ _   _ _ _ _
N Z B B   P Z C G     Z C   O V O R W

          E       E A   E
_ _ _ _ ,   _ _ _ _   _ _ _ _ _ _ _
D K S R     I K X O   D O Y V O C B W

  E
_ _ _ _ _ _ _ _ _ _ .       —Henry Ward Beecher
E B O I I Z C J I
```

Journaling

ART	FOOD	REFLECTION
BRAIN DUMP	GRATITUDE	TRAVEL
BULLET	MINUTE	VIDEO
DAILY	MORNING PAGES	VISUAL
DIARY	PEN	WASHI
	READING	

Cryptogram Quote

<table>
<tr><td>A</td><td>B</td><td>C</td><td>D</td><td>E</td><td>F</td><td>G</td><td>H</td><td>I</td><td>J</td><td>K</td><td>L</td><td>M</td></tr>
<tr><td></td><td></td><td></td><td></td><td>K</td><td></td><td></td><td></td><td>T</td><td></td><td></td><td></td><td></td></tr>
<tr><td>N</td><td>O</td><td>P</td><td>Q</td><td>R</td><td>S</td><td>T</td><td>U</td><td>V</td><td>W</td><td>X</td><td>Y</td><td>Z</td></tr>
<tr><td></td><td></td><td></td><td></td><td></td><td></td><td></td><td></td><td></td><td></td><td></td><td></td><td></td></tr>
</table>

```
          E                        E
  F  M  L  O     U  K  I  L  Z  L  O  K  U

     I     I     E     E
  I  Z  T  X  T  W  B  K     E  Z  P  C

  E        I     E     E           I
  K  G  O  T  O  W  K  C  K  G  O     T  U

                    I           E .
     B  Z  L  O  T  O  Q  A  K
```

— Brené Brown

If you could be one animal for the rest of your life, which would it be?

Learn to Meditate

STOERBL

RCTAEEH

NSUOD WOLB

PIOLWL

TENDTUS

IBVNTIORA

GNOG

LRSTCYA

Letter Circle

G I E
N Z R
C O E

Love of Country

ALLEGIANCE	HEROES	PATRIOTISM
COMMUNITY	HISTORY	PRIDE
CONFRONT	LOYALTY	PURSUIT
FREEDOM	NATION	SPEECH
HAPPINESS	PATRIOT	

Cryptogram Quote

A	B	C	D	E	F	G	H	I	J	K	L	M
				S								

N	O	P	Q	R	S	T	U	V	W	X	Y	Z
					I							

"E _ _ _ _ _"   _ S   _   _ E _ S _ .
 S D J H O E   R I   X   M S X I T

—Buddhist Proverb

Cryptogram Quote

A	B	C	D	E	F	G	H	I	J	K	L	M

N	O	P	Q	R	S	T	U	V	W	X	Y	Z
Q											K	

```
     N
_ _ _ _ _ _ _   _ _ _ _ _ _ _ _ _
L I X M Q A     Y B H A I A T O M

    N'                Y
_ _ _ _ _   _ _ _ _   _ _ _ _   _ _
I L Q A     S M B K   W T U D   A F

    N Y   N
_ _ _ _ _ _ _.
H Q K F Q M
```

—Gertrude Stein

Meditate Here

MRAHSA

AICRH

LSCAS

NDGEAR

RKAP

HEBNC

TTAERRE

YRAHPTE

Letter Circle

Visualization

ACHIEVEMENT	FUTURE	PERCEPT
DECISION	GOALS	PURPOSE
EXERCISE	GUIDED	RESOLUTION
EYES CLOSED	IMAGES	RESOLVE
FORMATION	MANIFEST	SENSES
	MIND	

Happy Scents

ISMJANE

CSIRUT

YNALG YLGAN

RSRAOEYM

NALILAV

THWEI MKSU

EBOTMGRA

IPNK PEPRPE

Letter Circle

 # Monthly Gratitude Reflections 

List five things you're grateful for this month:

1. ____

2. ____

3. ____

4. ____

5. ____

Write about one experience you had this month that you're especially grateful for:

List some people in your life that made you feel loved this month:

 # Monthly Plans and Goals 

List one big goal you'd like to accomplish this month:

____

____

____

____

What are some emotions you'd like to let go of this month?

-
-
-
-
-

What are some emotions you'd like to carry into this month?

-
-
-
-
-

Write some positive affirmations you can use throughout the month:

1. ____

2. ____

3. ____

Self-care Ideas

BATH	KINDNESS	SEW
CRAFT	MANICURE	SHOWER
DOG WALK	MASSAGE	SPA
EXERCISE	NAP	SUNRISE
HUG	PHONE OFF	THERAPY
	REST	

Cryptogram Quote

A	B	C	D	E	F	G	H	I	J	K	L	M
		N										

N	O	P	Q	R	S	T	U	V	W	X	Y	Z
					P							

```
       T       T
___  _  _  _  _  _  _  _  _  _    _  _  _
  R  J  I  P  D  P  F  E  S      I  L  E

     T     T  T        T
_  _  _  _  _  _  _  _      _  _  _      _  _  T
  I  P  P  D  P  F  E  S    I  J  S      L  T  P

C
_  _  _  _  _  _  _  _  _  _  _ ;    T  _  _  _  _      _  _  _
N  B  I  A  A  S  L  R  S  M      P  B  S  V        I  J  S

       C        C
_  _  _  _  _  _ .
N  B  T  D  N  S  M
```

—Robert Braathe

Monthly Vision Board

A vision board is a visual reminder of your goals and intentions. Inspire yourself and create a monthly vision board using this page to collage, doodle, sketch...or all of the above!

Praying

ERWNSA

REDESI

RILOPEM

RECETI

EUQSRET

TTUSR

UGRE

IMUBTS

Letter Circle

N T N
I C A
Z O G

Treat Yourself

BATH	FACIAL	ROOM SERVICE
BOUQUET	HOTEL	SHOPPING
COFFEE	MANICURE	SLEEP IN
DESSERT	MASSAGE	TEA
DRESS UP	PEDICURE	

Cryptogram Quote

A	B	C	D	E	F	G	H	I	J	K	L	M
O	D											

N	O	P	Q	R	S	T	U	V	W	X	Y	Z

```
    A        A          B        A
_ _____ _  _______  ___ _ _____
E  O Z     W O H H M   D I A O U B I

'        A              .  _  _____
E Z   L P O N I Q U S      E   A W T T B I

     B        A            .      A
__  __  ___________    ____
N T  D I  L P O N I Q U S    N W O N

   A                A
____________    ______  __
L P O N E N U K I   O S S T C B  Z I

     B        A
__  __  _______.
N T  D I  W O H H M
```

—Will Arnett

Write about where you live. Are you grateful to live there? Where else would you like to live and why?

Inner Peace

CPNACEEACT

NLABEAC

TONNTEC

EUATRGDTI

NAESPSHIP

LUGAH

TEAEITMD

PETSREC

Letter Circle

Cryptogram Quote

A	B	C	D	E	F	G	H	I	J	K	L	M

N	O	P	Q	R	S	T	U	V	W	X	Y	Z
				C		P						

```
        R
_ _ _ _ _ _   _ _   _ _ _ _
K R C Z U V   R Q   A Z T E

  _ _ _ _ _   _ _   _ _
  R F Z T Y K   R Q   L V

            U           R,      _ _ _
_ _ _ _ _ _ _ _   _ _ _   D T E
R F D T J A P G   A Q C

  U               R
_ _ _ _   _ _ _ _   _ _ _   _ _ _
B P K R   G Q Q J   A Q C   R F V

              U           R
_ _ _ _   _ _   _ _ _   _ _ _   _ _ _.
Y Q Q E   Z T   W F Q   X Q P   D C V
```

—Bethany Hamilton

275

Gratitude Quilt

BLOCK	PATCHWORK	SQUARE
EMBROIDER	PATTERN	STITCH
FABRIC	PERSONALIZE	STYLE
MAKE	SENTIMENTAL	WRITE

Peaceful Morning

RSISBDNOG

SARETBAFK

EEFFCO

EEECRIXS

IMUCS

YPRA

NISNHSEU

KALW

Letter Circle

Cryptogram Quote

<table>
<tr><td>A</td><td>B</td><td>C</td><td>D</td><td>E</td><td>F</td><td>G</td><td>H</td><td>I</td><td>J</td><td>K</td><td>L</td><td>M</td></tr>
<tr><td></td><td></td><td></td><td></td><td></td><td></td><td></td><td></td><td></td><td></td><td></td><td></td><td></td></tr>
<tr><td>N</td><td>O</td><td>P</td><td>Q</td><td>R</td><td>S</td><td>T</td><td>U</td><td>V</td><td>W</td><td>X</td><td>Y</td><td>Z</td></tr>
<tr><td></td><td></td><td></td><td></td><td></td><td>H</td><td></td><td></td><td></td><td></td><td></td><td>K</td><td></td></tr>
</table>

```
        Y                    Y
O X   V G B   R I N K   Z D P K B D

Y         S           S
K R U   H P O W   S P H   V G P I Q

  Y
K R U ,  V G P V   S R U N W   A B

B I R U M G .
```

— Meister Eckhart

Pure Imagination

CTNOEAIR

ATAFYNS

SLULONII

IRESPNI

IIVENETNV

NGTILYORIIA

ISOVNI

SRTAIT

Letter Circle

Cryptogram Quote

A	B	C	D	E	F	G	H	I	J	K	L	M

N	O	P	Q	R	S	T	U	V	W	X	Y	Z
						Y		Z				

W_ _ W_ _ _ _ _ W_ _ _ _ _ _ _ _ _
Z I Z J X W F Z J S S T W I B B

_ _ W_ _ _ _ _ _ _ _ _ _ _ _ _.
Q U Z I K S H Q B I F O J S I

T_ _ _ _ _ _ _ _ _ _ _ _ _ T_ _ _
Y P H R C B E Q M Q R E Q B Y P I

_ _ _ _ _ _ _ _ _ _ T_ _ _ T_
I R I O T J U F Q B L J R Y I R Y

_ _ _ _ _ _ _ _ T_ _ _ _ _ T_ _ _.
H R F F Q B B H Y Q B U H L Y Q J R

—Harry A. Ironside

Peaceful Evening

CUP OF TEA	LIGHT CANDLE	TAKE BATH
DIFFUSE OILS	MAKE DINNER	TIDY
FACE MASK	MEAL PREP	TURN DOWN LIGHTS
HYDRATE	NO SCREENS	WATCH TV
JOURNAL	PAJAMAS	YOGA
	SKINCARE	

 # Monthly Gratitude Reflections 

List five things you're grateful for this month:

1. ____

2. ____

3. ____

4. ____

5. ____

Write about one experience
you had this month that you're
especially grateful for:

List some people in your life that
made you feel loved this month:

Write a letter to someone you've always wanted to thank for their impact in your life.

Solutions

Page 5

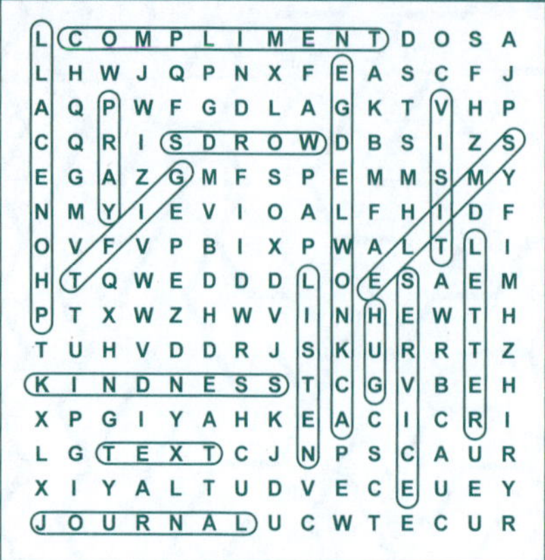

Page 10

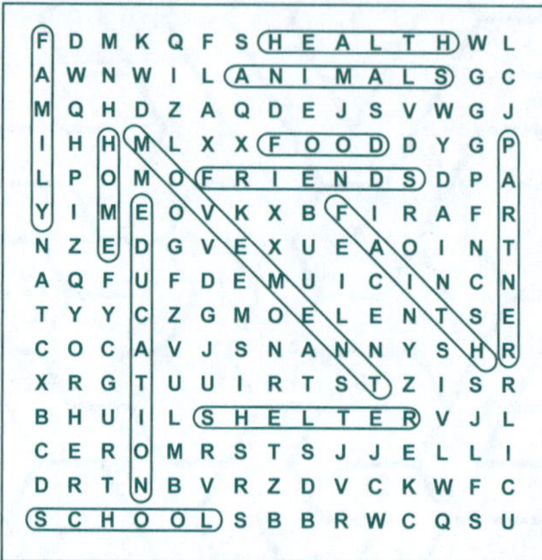

Page 6

A	B	C	D	E	F	G	H	I	J	K	L	M
D	E	G	R	A	P	Q	B	Y	O	C	L	U
N	O	P	Q	R	S	T	U	V	W	X	Y	Z
S	T	X	K	J	N	M	I	F	H	Z	V	W

True forgiveness is when you can say, "Thank you for the experience."

Page 7
Calming Instruments
chime, flute, guitar, harp, piano, singing bowl, triangle, ukulele

Letter Circle
GRATITUDE
There are about 25 words to find.

Page 8

Page 11

A	B	C	D	E	F	G	H	I	J	K	L	M
H	O	R	M	X	D	W	A	Q	F	E	L	C
N	O	P	Q	R	S	T	U	V	W	X	Y	Z
V	B	U	S	I	K	J	G	N	P	T	Y	Z

We should certainly count our blessings, but we should also make our blessings count.

Page 12
A Good Night's Sleep
down comforter, pajamas, melatonin, lavender, dreams, silk sheets, routine, white noise

Letter Circle
HAPPINESS
There are about 32 words to find.

Solutions

Page 16
Nature Walk
collect, creek, grass, identify, hike, leaves, meadow, birds

Letter Circle
MINDFUL
There are about 10 words to find.

Page 17

Page 19
Comforts of Home
running water, air conditioning, appliances, bathroom, family, heat, electricity, shower

Letter Circle
GRATEFUL
There are about 41 words to find.

Page 20

Page 21

A	B	C	D	E	F	G	H	I	J	K	L	M
G	L	K	O	Z	R	C	I	B	Q	D	P	X
N	O	P	Q	R	S	T	U	V	W	X	Y	Z
W	H	J	Y	V	U	A	M	T	S	E	F	N

Gratitude is not only the greatest of virtues, but the parent of all others.

Page 22

291

Solutions

Page 23
Memory Lane
dreaming, nostalgia, remember, ponder, recall, reminisce, revisit, flashback

Letter Circle
THANKFUL
There are about 15 words to find.

Page 24
Journal Here
apartment, backyard, bedroom, couch, table, kitchen, library, online

Letter Circle
EASYGOING
There are about 38 words to find.

Page 25

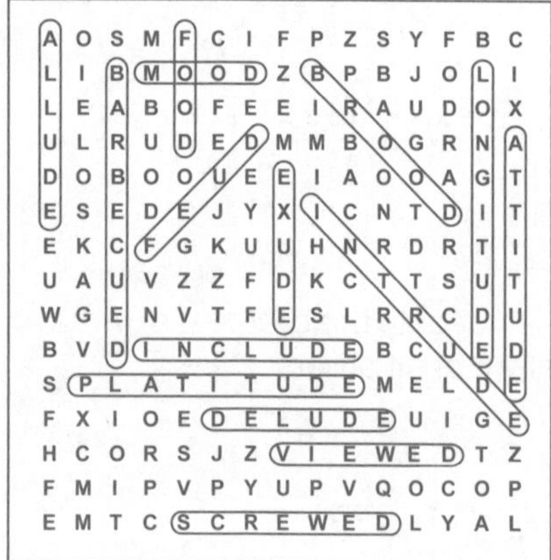

Page 26

A	B	C	D	E	F	G	H	I	J	K	L	M
A	B	I	J	G	O	H	N	M	R	P	S	F
N	O	P	Q	R	S	T	U	V	W	X	Y	Z
X	V	K	Z	T	W	E	Q	Y	C	U	D	L

Wear gratitude like a cloak, and it will feed every corner of your life.

Page 30

Page 31
Opposite of Stress
accept, comfort, consolation, disregard, endure, minimization, relax, understate

Letter Circle
CREATIVE
There are about 12 words to find.

Page 32
Self-actualization
accomplish, drive, fulfill, growth, maslow, potential, reach, realization

Letter Circle
ENERGETIC
There are about 15 words to find.

Page 34

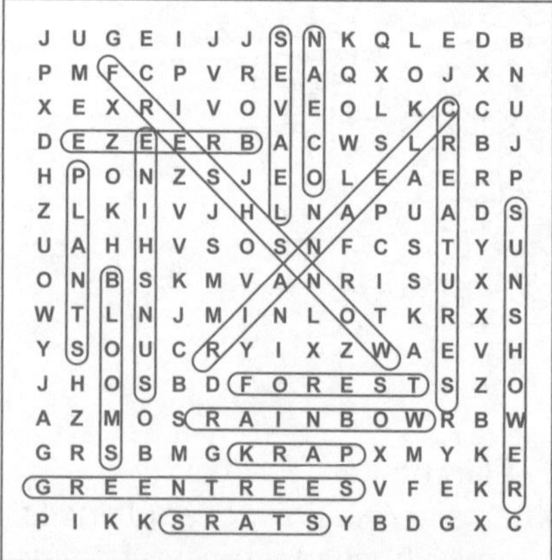

Solutions

Page 35

A	B	C	D	E	F	G	H	I	J	K	L	M
W	H	R	M	K	J	D	Y	I	Q	P	S	C
N	O	P	Q	R	S	T	U	V	W	X	Y	Z
Z	L	B	A	G	X	U	E	F	O	V	N	T

"Thank you" is the best prayer that anyone could say.

Page 36
Types of Dreams
daydream, falling, flying, being late, naked, nightmare, premonition, taking test

Letter Circle
HOPEFUL
There are about 10 words to find.

Page 37

Page 40

A	B	C	D	E	F	G	H	I	J	K	L	M
Q	Y	C	D	L	S	Z	M	H	I	X	N	T
N	O	P	Q	R	S	T	U	V	W	X	Y	Z
E	F	O	V	G	K	B	R	A	U	P	W	J

The soul that gives thanks can find comfort in everything; the soul that complains can find comfort in nothing.

Page 41

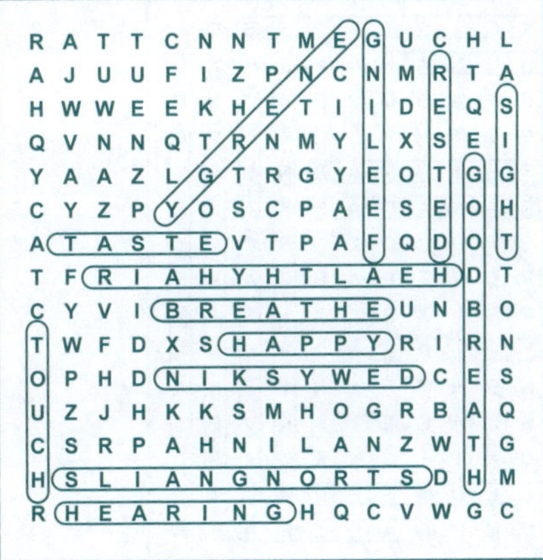

Page 42
Have a Grateful Day
deep breath, make bed, gratitude list, observe, nourish, shower, forgive, go walk

Letter Circle
MINDSET
There are about 35 words to find.

Page 43

Solutions

Page 44

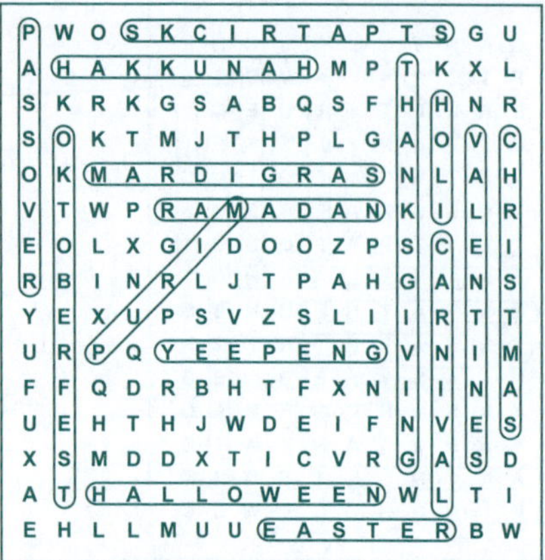

Page 49

Page 45

A	B	C	D	E	F	G	H	I	J	K	L	M
A	N	B	C	S	P	Y	V	I	Z	J	T	O

N	O	P	Q	R	S	T	U	V	W	X	Y	Z
U	K	W	G	M	D	Q	F	L	E	H	R	X

Gratitude is a big thing. It puts you in a place where you're humble.

Page 50

A	B	C	D	E	F	G	H	I	J	K	L	M
R	A	H	L	N	I	M	V	Q	B	F	C	D

N	O	P	Q	R	S	T	U	V	W	X	Y	Z
J	X	S	U	T	W	P	Z	G	Y	K	E	O

There's nothing nicer than unexpected appreciation. If you're grateful, get a pen.

Page 47
Mindfulness
conscious, listen, meditate, patience, pause, peace, present, sacred

Letter Circle
POSITIVITY
There are about 15 words to find.

Page 48
Magnificent Sky
cerulean, yellow, sherbet, orange, pink, rosy, cotton candy, lilac

Letter Circle
RELIEVED
There are about 30 words to find.

Page 53

Solutions

Page 54

Page 55
Self-care Kit
cozy socks, e-reader, face mask, journal, soft music, blanket, yoga mat, book

Letter Circle
PEACEFUL
There are about 15 words to find.

Page 56

A	B	C	D	E	F	G	H	I	J	K	L	M
D	I	N	W	L	G	E	J	F	C	O	K	B

N	O	P	Q	R	S	T	U	V	W	X	Y	Z
U	Y	H	A	Q	R	Z	S	V	X	M	P	T

Gratitude goes beyond the "mine" and "thine" and claims the truth that all of life is a pure gift.

Page 58
Stay in the Present
being, breathing, current, existent, mindful, observe, today, living

Letter Circle
DELIGHTED
There are about 20 words to find.

Page 59

Page 60

Page 61

A	B	C	D	E	F	G	H	I	J	K	L	M
E	N	X	H	S	Y	V	Q	I	A	F	B	G

N	O	P	Q	R	S	T	U	V	W	X	Y	Z
C	T	D	P	R	Z	O	J	U	K	W	M	L

When eating fruit, remember the one who planted the tree.

Solutions

Page 64
Rhymes with Chill
daffodil, drill, instill, fulfill, molehill, tranquil, windmill, refill

Letter Circle
PLEASED
There are about 40 words to find.

Page 65

A	B	C	D	E	F	G	H	I	J	K	L	M
A	Z	V	O	X	Q	T	D	F	U	E	P	B

N	O	P	Q	R	S	T	U	V	W	X	Y	Z
C	N	M	K	Y	S	W	H	J	R	L	G	I

Gratitude is the ability to experience life as a gift. It liberates us from the prison of self-preoccupation.

Page 66

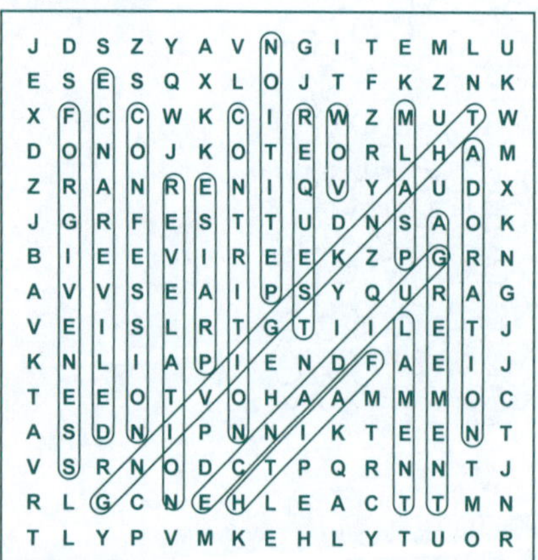

Page 67
Self-care Day
craft, massage, shower, therapy, bake, gardening, podcast, staycation

Letter Circle
GRATIFIED
There are about 45 words to find.

Page 68

Page 69

A	B	C	D	E	F	G	H	I	J	K	L	M
D	G	B	A	P	H	C	E	O	V	N	Y	X

N	O	P	Q	R	S	T	U	V	W	X	Y	Z
F	L	J	U	S	Z	R	W	Q	I	T	K	M

I awoke this morning with devout thanksgiving for my friends, the old and the new.

Page 71
Intuition
cognition, insight, instinct, knowledge, percept, premonition, rational, sense

Letter Circle
APPRECIATE
There are about 40 words to find.

Page 72

A	B	C	D	E	F	G	H	I	J	K	L	M
P	E	S	T	J	H	I	R	C	L	O	U	F

N	O	P	Q	R	S	T	U	V	W	X	Y	Z
N	M	A	V	X	Y	W	Z	G	Q	B	K	D

Piglet noticed that even though he had a Very Small Heart, it could hold a rather large amount of Gratitude.

Solutions

Page 73

Page 74
The Divine in Me...
namaste, hindu, honor, light, yoga,
subconscious, phrase, sanskrit

Letter Circle
THOUGHTFUL
There are about 15 words to find.

Page 77

Page 78

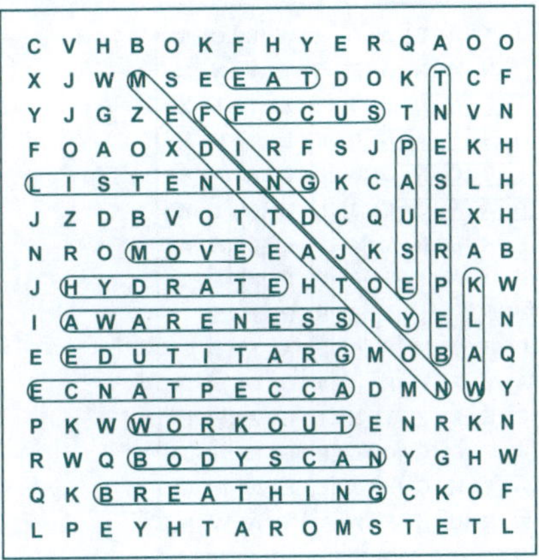

Page 79
Spa Day
facial, dry brush, masseuse, mud bath,
sauna, scrub, seaweed wrap, clay mask

Letter Circle
GRACIOUS
There are about 10 words to find.

Page 80

A	B	C	D	E	F	G	H	I	J	K	L	M
X	A	I	S	H	G	R	B	L	E	D	V	Y
N	O	P	Q	R	S	T	U	V	W	X	Y	Z
J	P	Z	F	N	M	C	U	K	O	T	W	Q

If you see no reason for giving thanks, the
fault lies only in yourself.

Page 82
Enlighten Me
absorb, awareness, cultivate, improve,
insight, perception, realize, knowledge

Letter Circle
MEDITATE
There are about 35 words to find.

Solutions

Page 83

Page 84

Page 85

As we express our gratitude, we must never forget that the highest appreciation is not to utter words, but to live by them.

Page 88
Peaceful Piano
bass string, hammer, keyboard, music shelf, sheet music, treble string, tuning pin, pedal

Letter Circle
CARING
There are about 10 words to find.

Page 89

Gratitude is the sign of noble souls.

Page 90

Page 91
Rhymes with Mind
behind, declined, dined, grind, lined, signed, whined, wined

Letter Circle
INTUITIVE
There are about 15 words to find.

Solutions

Page 92

Page 93

A	B	C	D	E	F	G	H	I	J	K	L	M
M	I	X	H	W	O	F	L	B	N	G	S	Z
N	O	P	Q	R	S	T	U	V	W	X	Y	Z
U	D	E	Q	R	C	V	P	J	K	A	T	Y

This is a wonderful day. I have never seen this one before.

Page 95
Wide-open Windows
breeze, curtain, glass, drape, singing, nature, picture, sunlight

Letter Circle
THERAPY
There are about 43 words to find.

Page 96

A	B	C	D	E	F	G	H	I	J	K	L	M
C	Y	W	V	B	R	M	T	L	J	Q	F	D
N	O	P	Q	R	S	T	U	V	W	X	Y	Z
P	H	A	K	I	Z	O	N	X	E	S	G	U

Acknowledging the good that you already have in your life is the foundation for all abundance.

Page 97

Page 98
Mood-boosting Colors
butter yellow, hot pink, fern green, orange, deep purple, coastal blue, mint green, sunrise orange

Letter Circle
WISDOM
There are about 10 words to find.

Page 101

Solutions

Page 102

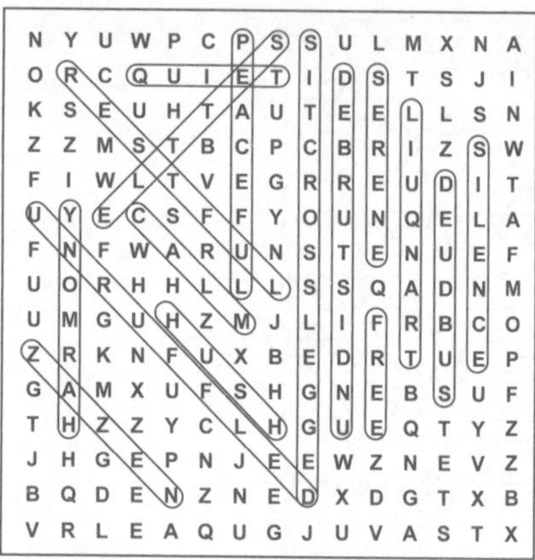

Page 103
Rhymes with Peace
crease, eyepiece, fleece, geese, grease, decrease, niece, police

Letter Circle
REFLECTION
There are about 40 words to find.

Page 104

A	B	C	D	E	F	G	H	I	J	K	L	M
O	M	J	P	T	A	B	Z	U	Q	V	C	W
N	O	P	Q	R	S	T	U	V	W	X	Y	Z
D	L	N	E	F	X	Y	G	S	R	H	I	K

Live a life full of humility, gratitude, intellectual curiosity, and never stop learning.

Page 106
Places to Puzzle
bedroom, cabin, coffee table, hotel, school, table, waiting room, floor

Letter Circle
SERENELY
There are about 17 words to find.

Page 107

Page 108

Page 109
Quiet Time
hushed, low talking, muffled, restful, tranquil, whisper, speechless, silence

Letter Circle
PLEASANT
There are about 125 words to find.

Solutions

Page 112
Tranquil Plants
aloe, bamboo, bonsai, moss, peace lily, willow tree, wisteria, snake

Letter Circle
FEELINGS
There are about 30 words to find.

Page 113

A	B	C	D	E	F	G	H	I	J	K	L	M
D	W	S	F	R	N	V	I	J	A	K	Z	Q

N	O	P	Q	R	S	T	U	V	W	X	Y	Z
E	O	B	T	L	C	H	P	X	G	M	U	Y

Gratitude is riches. Complaint is poverty.

Page 114

Page 115
Self-care Night
bath, meditate, stretch, read, snack, sleep, cuddle, movie

Letter Circle
SENTIMENT
There are about 25 words to find.

Page 116

Page 117

A	B	C	D	E	F	G	H	I	J	K	L	M
A	B	P	R	N	C	T	O	G	J	W	H	E

N	O	P	Q	R	S	T	U	V	W	X	Y	Z
S	D	L	U	I	F	M	V	X	Z	Y	K	Q

I lie in bed at night, after ending my prayers with the words: Thank you, God, for all that is good and dear and beautiful.

Page 119
Peaceful Personalities
collected, harmonious, restful, serene, smooth, soothing, tranquil, unbothered

Letter Circle
SWEETNESS
There are about 26 words to find.

Page 120

A	B	C	D	E	F	G	H	I	J	K	L	M
A	V	B	C	D	W	X	M	E	Q	T	P	J

N	O	P	Q	R	S	T	U	V	W	X	Y	Z
R	F	S	L	G	O	N	K	H	U	Y	I	Z

Who does not thank for little will not thank for much.

Solutions

Page 121

Page 122
Rhymes with Care
bare, chair, flair, glare, scare, snare, wear, spare

Letter Circle
PASSION
There are about 30 words to find.

Page 125

Page 126

A	B	C	D	E	F	G	H	I	J	K	L	M
D	A	C	B	I	R	G	S	H	N	V	E	J
N	O	P	Q	R	S	T	U	V	W	X	Y	Z
O	T	P	K	M	Y	F	Z	Q	L	U	W	X

We learned about gratitude and humility—that so many people had a hand in our success.

Page 127
Meditation Vibes
breathe, contemplate, dream, explore, mantra, ponder, present, reflect

Letter Circle
SPIRITED
There are about 68 words to find.

Page 128

Solutions

Page 130

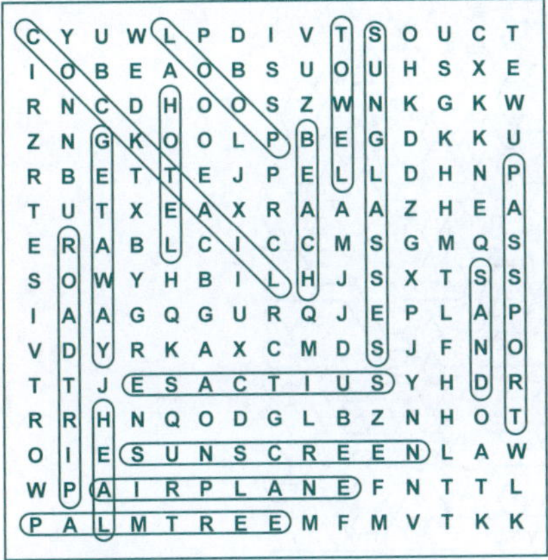

Page 133

Page 131

A	B	C	D	E	F	G	H	I	J	K	L	M
F	E	W	O	I	A	J	G	N	Q	R	S	X
N	O	P	Q	R	S	T	U	V	W	X	Y	Z
L	D	K	T	Y	H	V	U	P	B	C	M	Z

Gratitude looks to the Past and love to the Present; fear, avarice, lust, and ambition look ahead.

Page 132
Grateful Spirit

attitude, essence, identity, mindset, perspective, soul, being, belief

Letter Circle
VITALITY
There are about 10 words to find.

Page 136
Watch the Sunrise

blanket, coffee, camera, daybreak, view, sunglasses, picnic, thermos

Letter Circle
PSYCHE
There are about 10 words to find.

Page 137

303

Solutions

Page 139
Breathwork
abdominal, belly, count, deep breath, exercise, focus, nostril, diaphragm

Letter Circle
ESSENCE
There are about 10 words to find.

Page 140

Page 141

A	B	C	D	E	F	G	H	I	J	K	L	M
D	A	X	F	G	I	L	E	B	S	V	T	O
N	O	P	Q	R	S	T	U	V	W	X	Y	Z
C	U	R	Q	M	H	Z	P	J	Y	K	N	W

I'm still thanking all the stars, one by one.

Page 142

Page 143
Intentions for Spring
abundance, change, cleanse, nurture, rebirth, refresh, welcome, plant

Letter Circle
MANIFEST
There are about 30 words to find.

Page 144
Mindfulness Types
body scan, breathing, mantra, meditation, movement, stretch, visualization, yoga

Letter Circle
SOULFUL
There are about 10 words to find.

Solutions

Page 145

Page 146

A	B	C	D	E	F	G	H	I	J	K	L	M
X	A	M	S	B	I	Z	U	W	H	F	K	R
N	O	P	Q	R	S	T	U	V	W	X	Y	Z
E	V	Y	D	P	N	C	L	Q	J	G	O	T

For me, every house is grace. And I feel gratitude in my heart each time I can meet someone and look at his or her smile.

Page 149
Grateful Animals

dogs, chimpanzee, turkey, impala, vampire bat, cats, dolphin, elephant

Letter Circle
WARMING
There are about 20 words to find.

Page 150

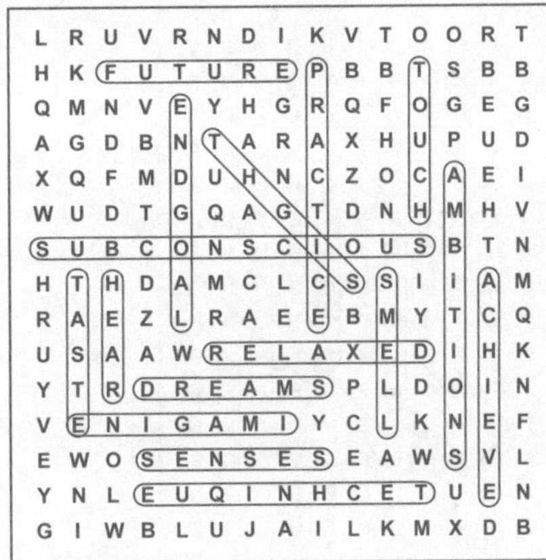

Page 152
Rhymes with Love

dove, hereof, ladylove, shove, thereof, above, glove, sort of

Letter Circle
HEARTFELT
There are about 30 words to find.

Page 154

A	B	C	D	E	F	G	H	I	J	K	L	M
S	Y	H	V	M	E	X	W	L	U	T	R	O
N	O	P	Q	R	S	T	U	V	W	X	Y	Z
G	B	A	F	D	P	I	N	Z	K	C	Q	J

No duty is more urgent than giving thanks.

Solutions

Page 155

Page 156

Page 157

A	B	C	D	E	F	G	H	I	J	K	L	M
A	V	D	F	S	X	Z	H	J	U	P	C	B

N	O	P	Q	R	S	T	U	V	W	X	Y	Z
L	G	K	E	I	W	N	M	R	O	Q	T	Y

Enjoy the little things, for one day you may look back and realize they were the big things.

Page 160
Faith Words
believe, devotion, hope, love, reliance, trust, worship, profess

Letter Circle
GENUINE
There are about 10 words to find.

Page 161

Page 162

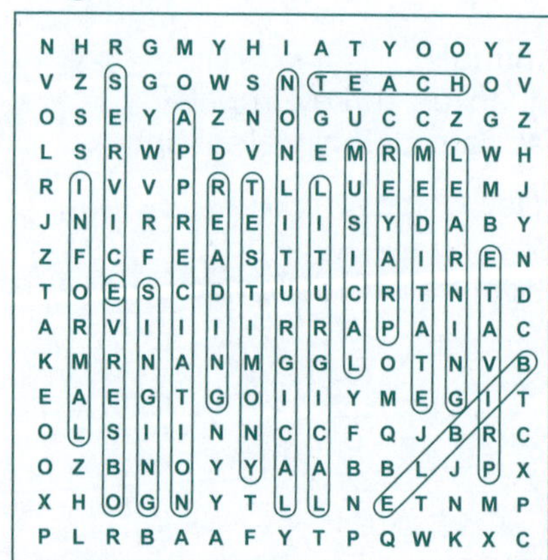

Solutions

Page 163

A	B	C	D	E	F	G	H	I	J	K	L	M
P	X	H	G	J	O	I	Q	U	T	C	Z	K

N	O	P	Q	R	S	T	U	V	W	X	Y	Z
B	D	L	W	Y	S	E	F	A	M	R	V	N

We must find time to stop and thank the people who make a difference in our lives.

Page 164

A	B	C	D	E	F	G	H	I	J	K	L	M
S	J	D	T	A	H	Y	X	I	Q	V	Z	R

N	O	P	Q	R	S	T	U	V	W	X	Y	Z
P	N	L	K	B	U	C	M	F	W	G	O	E

I would maintain that thanks are the highest form of thought; and that gratitude is happiness doubled by wonder.

Page 165
Night Sky

starry, twilight, nightfall, heavens, dusk, celestial, lunar, inky

Letter Circle
HEARTENS
There are about 60 words to find.

Page 166

Page 167

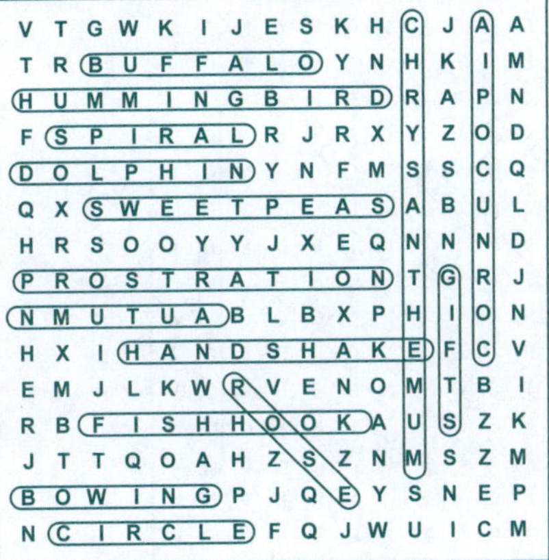

Page 168
Stress Relief

acupuncture, breathe, connect, counseling, laugh, massage, music, therapy

Letter Circle
SINCERE
There are about 20 words to find.

Page 171

Solutions

Page 172

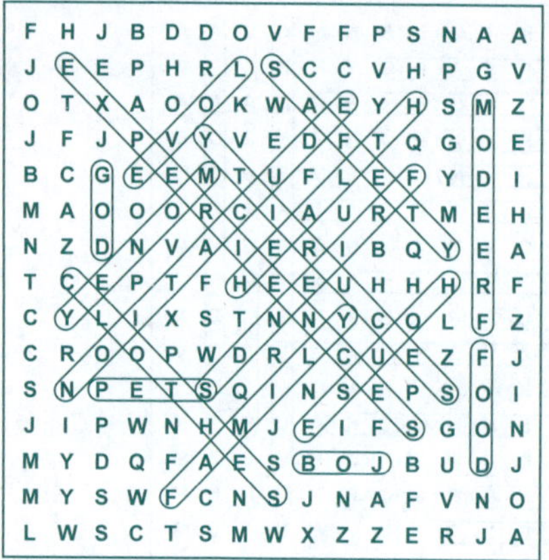

Page 173
Deep Conversation
banter, chitchat, converse, deliberate, discourse, exchange, vulnerable, share

Letter Circle
GENEROUS
There are about 44 words to find.

Page 174

A	B	C	D	E	F	G	H	I	J	K	L	M
E	Z	K	U	D	J	F	L	W	C	T	Y	B
N	O	P	Q	R	S	T	U	V	W	X	Y	Z
X	R	N	Q	A	S	I	G	H	P	V	O	M

The deepest craving of human nature is the need to be appreciated.

Page 176
Peaceful Animals
butterfly, crane, dove, horse, kingfisher, manatee, panda, sloth

Letter Circle
KINDNESS
There are about 30 words to find.

Page 177

Page 178

Page 179

A	B	C	D	E	F	G	H	I	J	K	L	M
H	A	E	V	Q	T	X	B	L	K	P	R	M
N	O	P	Q	R	S	T	U	V	W	X	Y	Z
J	Y	C	O	U	Z	G	D	S	N	F	I	W

When I started counting my blessings, my whole life turned around.

Solutions

Page 182
Intentions for Winter
joyful, calm, commit, connect, coziness, understand, reflect, heal

Letter Circle
BLESSING
There are about 30 words to find.

Page 183

A	B	C	D	E	F	G	H	I	J	K	L	M
A	E	D	J	O	N	H	P	W	Y	M	I	C

N	O	P	Q	R	S	T	U	V	W	X	Y	Z
L	X	G	V	S	B	K	U	F	R	Z	T	Q

Gratitude bestows reverence…changing forever how we experience life and the world.

Page 184

Page 185
Cuddle Up
swaddle, weighted blanket, comforter, baby, heating pad, partner, sleeping bag, stuffed animal

Letter Circle
GRACEFUL
There are about 25 words to find.

Page 186

Page 187

A	B	C	D	E	F	G	H	I	J	K	L	M
M	E	S	T	K	W	D	A	J	N	G	R	B

N	O	P	Q	R	S	T	U	V	W	X	Y	Z
Q	X	F	Y	I	C	Z	H	L	O	U	V	P

Always have an attitude of gratitude.

Page 189
Get Outside
bird-watch, beekeeping, garden, photograph, rockpooling, stargaze, hiking, picnic

Letter Circle
BLISSFUL
There are about 10 words to find.

Page 190

A	B	C	D	E	F	G	H	I	J	K	L	M
P	W	M	D	U	B	F	I	L	S	G	Z	H

N	O	P	Q	R	S	T	U	V	W	X	Y	Z
Q	A	N	Y	C	T	R	E	J	X	O	V	K

Rest and be thankful.

Solutions

Page 191

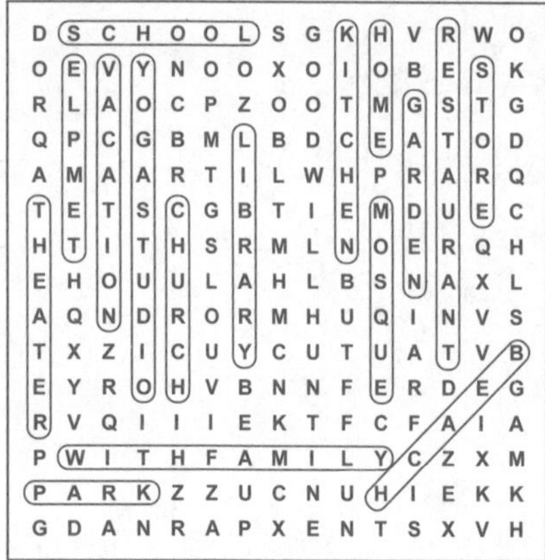

Page 196

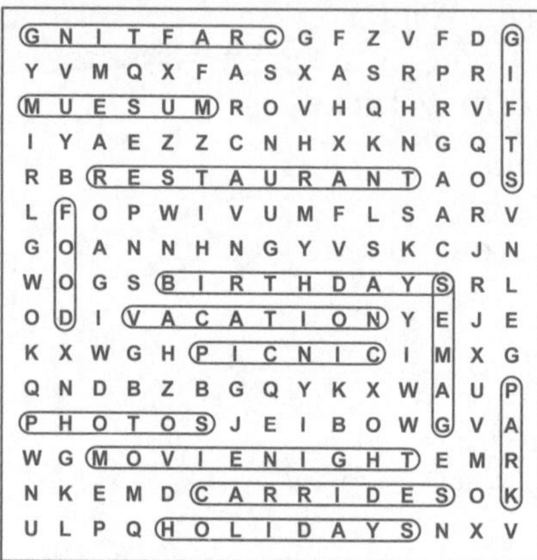

Page 192
Rhymes with Calm
qualm, psalm, embalm, Islam, bomb, balm, prom, palm

Letter Circle
JOYOUS
There are about 9 words to find.

Page 195
Keep a Calm Home
candle, color, aromatherapy, open window, declutter, good flow, lighting, soothing sounds

Letter Circle
SUNNILY
There are about 10 words to find.

Page 198
Happy Words
chirpy, glee, jolly, peppy, shining, summery, sparkling, tickled

Letter Circle
CHEERFUL
There are about 10 words to find.

Page 200

A	B	C	D	E	F	G	H	I	J	K	L	M
Y	X	W	B	U	A	K	P	J	H	Z	T	D
N	O	P	Q	R	S	T	U	V	W	X	Y	Z
O	F	I	N	M	C	S	E	L	Q	V	R	G

Gratitude is a powerful catalyst for happiness. It's the spark that lights a fire of joy in your soul.

Solutions

Page 201

Page 202

Page 203

A	B	C	D	E	F	G	H	I	J	K	L	M
F	G	K	I	O	R	Z	M	A	H	B	V	U
N	O	P	Q	R	S	T	U	V	W	X	Y	Z
C	X	W	T	J	P	N	Y	E	L	Q	D	S

Let us be grateful to the people who make us happy; they are the charming gardeners who make our souls blossom.

Page 206
Glass Half Full
cheery, creative, energetic, happy, hopeful, mindset, optimism, positive

Letter Circle
AMUSING
There are about 19 words to find.

Page 207

Page 208

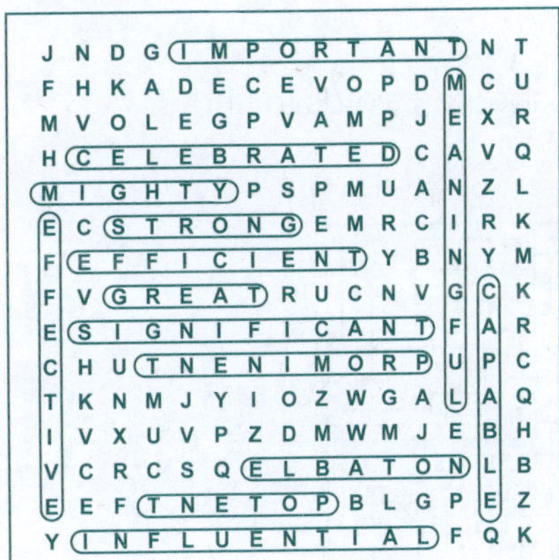

Solutions

Page 209

A	B	C	D	E	F	G	H	I	J	K	L	M
V	Z	A	W	B	O	Y	F	C	R	D	M	Q
N	O	P	Q	R	S	T	U	V	W	X	Y	Z
P	K	E	X	G	T	H	N	J	I	S	U	L

We can only be said to be alive in those moments when our hearts are conscious of our treasures.

Page 210

A	B	C	D	E	F	G	H	I	J	K	L	M
A	D	F	J	C	Z	X	Y	I	H	K	V	O
N	O	P	Q	R	S	T	U	V	W	X	Y	Z
L	M	E	N	U	R	T	P	G	S	W	B	Q

Got no checkbooks, got no banks, still I'd like to express my thanks. I got the sun in the morning and the moon at night.

Page 211
Grounding
connection, charge, earth, foundation, land, practice, stand, soil

Letter Circle
HAPPILY
There are about 15 words to find.

Page 212

Page 213

Page 214
Mood-boosting Herbs
rhodiola, holy basil, licorice, ginseng, lemon balm, ashwagandha, rose, cinnamon

Letter Circle
MELLOWED
There are about 24 words to find.

Page 218

Solutions

Page 219
Breakfast in Bed
bacon, bagel, coffee, french toast, frittata, toast, oatmeal, scone

Letter Circle
EUPHORIC
There are about 15 words to find.

Page 220
Bath Essentials
caddy, candle, diffuser, rubber duck, towel, wine, washcloth, spa pillow

Letter Circle
ELATEDLY
There are about 15 words to find.

Page 222

Page 223

Joy is the simplest form of gratitude.

Page 224
#Goals
career, educational, family, financial, fitness, health, personal, relationship

Letter Circle
EXUBERANT
There are about 10 words to find.

Page 225

Page 228

When we focus on our gratitude, the tide of disappointment goes out and the tide of love rushes in.

Solutions

Page 229

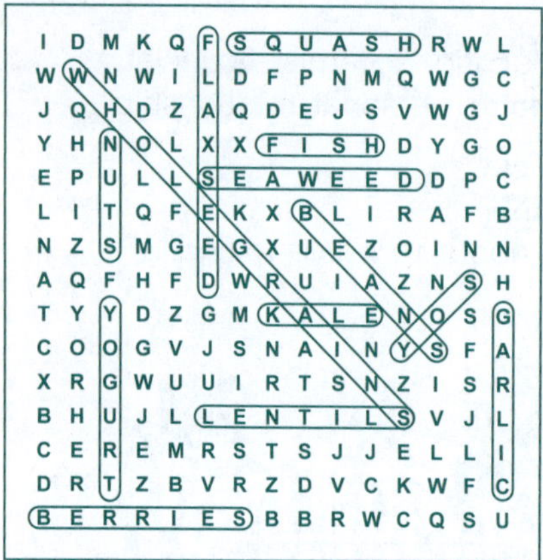

Page 230
Mindful Puzzles

anagram, crossword, cryptogram, jigsaw, logic, maze, riddle, word search

Letter Circle
RADIANT
There are about 15 words to find.

Page 231

Page 232

Page 233

A	B	C	D	E	F	G	H	I	J	K	L	M
B	K	X	W	U	N	H	Y	G	C	M	S	J
N	O	P	Q	R	S	T	U	V	W	X	Y	Z
Q	F	V	I	E	D	Z	L	P	R	T	A	O

When it comes to life the critical thing is whether you take things for granted or take them with gratitude.

Page 235
Moon Ritual

offering, corn, feminine energy, full moon, goddess, worship, release, harvest

Letter Circle
GLOWING
There are about 15 words to find.

Page 236
Body Scan

insight, release, self-compassion, guided, tension, sensation, meditation

Letter Circle
INDEBTED
There are about 20 words to find.

Solutions

Page 237

Page 242

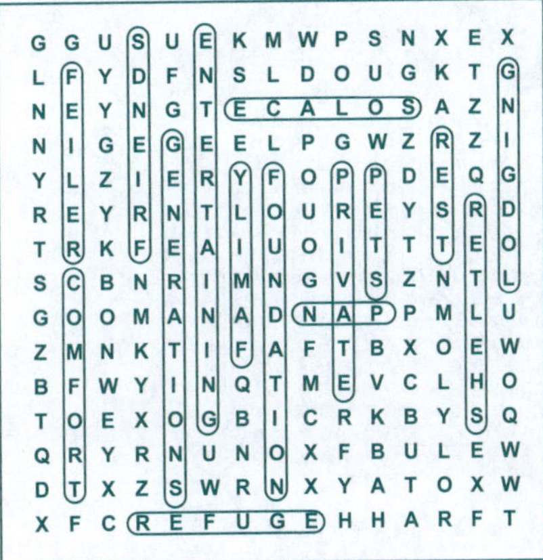

Page 238

O Lord that lends me life, lend me a heart replete with thankfulness.

Page 241
Loving Kindness
amity, chant, compassion, embody, good will, meditate, radical, sublime state

Letter Circle
SATISFIED
There are about 20 words to find.

Page 244
Energy Balancing
blocked, centers, chakra, expend, healing, strength, state, intake

Letter Circle
KNOWLEDGE
There are about 36 words to find.

Page 246

The unthankful heart discovers no mercies; but the thankful heart will find, in every hour, some heavenly blessings.

Solutions

Page 247

Page 248

Page 249

A	B	C	D	E	F	G	H	I	J	K	L	M
L	V	H	A	K	E	B	M	T	J	D	W	C
N	O	P	Q	R	S	T	U	V	W	X	Y	Z
G	P	I	Y	Z	U	O	Q	X	F	S	N	R

What separates privilege from entitlement is gratitude.

Page 252

Learn to Meditate

bolster, teacher, sound bowl, pillow, student, vibration, gong, crystal

Letter Circle

RECOGNIZE

There are about 10 words to find.

Page 253

Page 254

Solutions

Page 255

A B C D E F G H I J K L M
X K G Q S M O E R A P U Z
N O P Q R S T U V W X Y Z
D J N W Y I T H L B V F C

"Enough" is a feast.

Page 256

A B C D E F G H I J K L M
H E U O M P Y D I Z C X W
N O P Q R S T U V W X Y Z
Q F J R B L A T S V G K N

Silent gratitude isn't very much to anyone.

Page 257
Meditate Here
ashram, chair, class, garden, park, bench, retreat, therapy

Letter Circle
GRATEFULLY
There are about 30 words to find.

Page 258

Page 259

Page 260
Happy Scents
jasmine, citrus, ylang ylang, rosemary, vanilla, white musk, bergamot, pink pepper

Letter Circle
TRIBUTE
There are about 10 words to find.

Page 263

Solutions

Page 264

Page 266

A	B	C	D	E	F	G	H	I	J	K	L	M
I	Q	N	E	S	G	R	B	D	K	X	A	O

N	O	P	Q	R	S	T	U	V	W	X	Y	Z
L	T	W	U	J	M	P	F	Y	Z	H	V	C

Gratitude and attitude are not challenges; they are choices.

Page 268
Praying

answer, desire, implore, recite, request, trust, urge, submit

Letter Circle
COGNIZANT
There are about 25 words to find.

Page 269

Page 270

Page 271

A	B	C	D	E	F	G	H	I	J	K	L	M
O	D	A	K	I	Q	L	W	E	Y	V	S	Z

N	O	P	Q	R	S	T	U	V	W	X	Y	Z
G	T	H	X	P	B	N	U	F	C	J	M	R

I am happy because I'm grateful. I choose to be grateful. That gratitude allows me to be happy.

Solutions

Page 274
Inner Peace
acceptance, balance, content, gratitude, happiness, laugh, meditate, respect

Letter Circle
CONSCIOUS
There are about 15 words to find.

Page 275

A	B	C	D	E	F	G	H	I	J	K	L	M
D	L	I	E	V	A	Y	F	Z	B	J	G	O

N	O	P	Q	R	S	T	U	V	W	X	Y	Z
T	Q	M	N	C	K	R	P	U	W	H	X	S

Strive to find things to be thankful for, and just look for the good in who you are.

Page 276

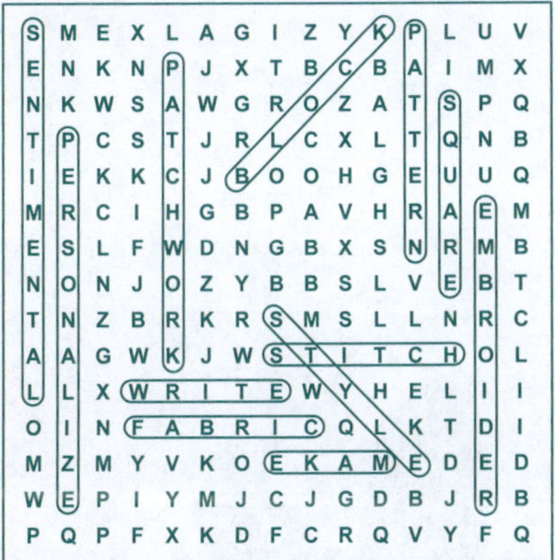

Page 277
Peaceful Morning
songbirds, breakfast, coffee, exercise, music, pray, sunshine, walk

Letter Circle
OBSERVANT
There are about 25 words to find.

Page 278

Page 279

A	B	C	D	E	F	G	H	I	J	K	L	M
P	A	L	W	B	X	M	G	O	J	Q	N	C

N	O	P	Q	R	S	T	U	V	W	X	Y	Z
I	R	Z	T	D	H	V	U	E	S	F	K	Y

If the only prayer you said was thank you, that would be enough.

Page 281
Pure Imagination
creation, fantasy, illusion, inspire, inventive, originality, vision, artist

Letter Circle
ATTENTIVE
There are about 20 words to find.

Page 282

A	B	C	D	E	F	G	H	I	J	K	L	M
H	G	L	F	I	U	E	P	Q	D	C	W	O

N	O	P	Q	R	S	T	U	V	W	X	Y	Z
R	J	K	V	S	B	Y	X	M	Z	A	T	N

We would worry less if we praised more. Thanksgiving is the enemy of discontent and dissatisfaction.

Solutions

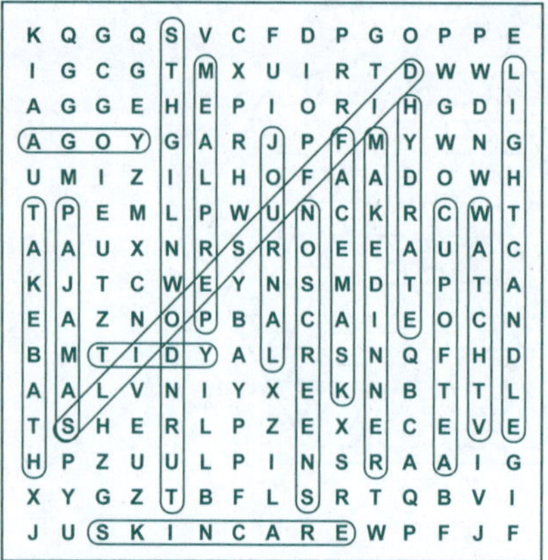